The Instruction Manual

for College Papers

The Instruction Manual for College Papers

An Easy Step-by-Step Guide to Writing Quality Essays

Danalynn Coulon
Edited by Christopher Coulon

ISBN-13: 978-1492853220
ISBN-10: 1492853224

Table of Contents

Introduction

The cursor blinks, the blank document shining a condemning white light in your eyes. You shuffle through your papers, eyes drifting across the text without processing any of the information, turning to re-read the prompt yet again. The document remains relentlessly blank.

Does this sound familiar? Often starting a paper is the most challenging step, but it is also the most important. The initial process can either guide you toward a well-ordered paper or mislead you to one with no direction.

As a long-time student, I know what it's like to be on that side of the desk. I clearly remember the curling feeling of dread deep within my abdomen when a paper has been put off to the last minute and a masterpiece must be cranked out overnight. However, I have the advantage of sitting on the other side of the desk as well. I have reviewed thousands of essays, written tens of thousands of recommendations for improvement and I have seen the most common difficulties that students face when writing a paper. When I create writing prompts, I am distinctly aware of what each turn of phrase implies. These perspectives, as a student and educator, have been combined while writing this book.

When you have multiple commitments pulling you back and forth, you do not want to spend more time than necessary to produce a quality paper. I have spent years collecting tips and refining a linear, step-by-step plan to writing a paper with the fewest major revisions and the least wasted time. This process has been tested for over seven years by the students I have helped in crafting high achieving papers. The steps I have laid out will carry you all the way from reading the prompt to putting the finishing touches on your paper.

This book is laid out as an outline of sequential tasks, leading you through the writing process. Each chapter has a common theme and within the chapter are numbered steps to guide you through the process. This book is meant for you to follow along with a prompt in hand. Even if you are in the middle of drafting your paper, you can jump in at the chapter describing your next action or turn to a section that is giving you difficulty. Unlike other writing guides that give help mainly with the editing process, assuming you have a complete draft already, this book focuses on creating a solid rough draft. It is only after a strong rough draft has been created that the focus shifts to editing and formatting.

Chapter 1 starts off by analyzing and deciphering the prompt. There are three main categories of prompts: narrative, informative and persuasive. Writing a narrative style paper is a different process than the other two and is covered in Chapter 12. The brainstorming process is similar for all three styles and is covered in

Chapter 2.

The process of writing informative and persuasive style papers continues in Chapter 3, where you draft your thesis and look at the points you want your paper to focus on. In Chapter 4 you learn about and collect the different types of concrete details that you will need.

Chapter 5 turns the focus to writing commentary, followed by Chapter 6, which leads you through assembling the body paragraphs. Chapter 7 helps you to write your introduction, while Chapter 8 guides you in forming your conclusion. Chapter 9 continues by leading you through the process of properly citing sources. At this point, the first rough draft of the paper is complete. Editing takes place in Chapter 10, which addresses several easy grammatical fixes, and in Chapter 11, where you revise the formatting of your paper. Chapter 12 is devoted purely to writing a narrative style paper, as the process is different than that for writing an informative or persuasive style paper.

This may sound like a complicated process, but if you work on a paper while following along in the book, you will see that the step-by-step process outlined in this book is easy to follow. This book is organized to be used either while you are writing a paper or as a quick reference source. Before you dive into the paper-writing process itself, I strongly recommend reading through the following section, "The Examples in This Book," to have a clearer understanding of the examples that I will be using throughout these steps.

Happy writing!

The Examples in This Book

To guide you through this paper-writing process, I have included two types of examples. The first type of example is simply meant to illustrate the concept being explained; this example is shown as an aside in a box with a white background.

The second type of example shows the development of a sample paper at each vital step. This "Example Throughout the Process" section is shown in a box with a light grey background. The final Example Throughout the Process papers, one persuasive and one narrative, can be found in Appendixes II and III.

All of the examples in this book will be focused on Jack London's short story "To Build a Fire" and its historical context. The full text of this story can be found in Appendix I; **I strongly encourage reviewing the short story before you begin reading this book to have a clearer understanding of the specific examples provided.**

Jack London was an American writer who lived from 1876-1916. He lived a rough life, working a variety of jobs including cannery worker, pirate, seal hunter, and gold prospector in the Yukon Gold Rush. The Yukon

Gold Rush, also known as the Klondike Gold Rush, started in 1897 with the news that people were finding a wealth of gold nuggets along the Klondike River near Yukon, Alaska. London tried his luck but was unsuccessful as a gold prospector. However, his experiences in the Yukon area provided material for many of his future stories, including *The Call of the Wild*, *White Fang*, and "To Build a Fire" (Streissguth).

"To Build a Fire" was published in 1908 and takes place during the Yukon Gold Rush. It is a short story about a man who attempts a solitary travel across a portion of the Yukon in extremely cold temperatures. The Man, who remains nameless throughout the story, ignores the advice of the Yukon veterans in town to never travel alone and is accompanied only by his dog. He ends up falling through ice into a stream, soaking his legs and feet. With no companion to come to his aid, he fails twice at making a successful fire and ends up freezing to death. This classic tale exemplifies the conflict between man and nature.

The Main Parts of an Essay

Body Paragraph: Paragraphs that form the bulk of your essay and are found between the introduction and the conclusion. The purpose of a body paragraph is to uphold and explain your thesis statement. Each body paragraph should have one main, unique idea around which it revolves, and the entire paragraph should directly support your thesis statement.

Commentary: Used to show why a concrete detail is relevant and how it supports the thesis. This is the chance for you to explain your thoughts and opinions.

Conclusion: The last paragraph or section in your paper; this is the place for you to wrap up your main ideas. The primary message should be reinforced here so the audience leaves with a clear idea of your paper's purpose.

Concrete Detail: Pieces of evidence used as support for your central argument. Concrete details may be facts, quotes, paraphrases or summaries.

Full Citation: A complete set of information for a source, found in the Works Cited section at the end of your paper. The way this information is written, and the exact information required, varies based on the writing style of the paper.

Hook: A short section at the beginning of the introduction which is meant to capture the reader's attention.

In-text Citation: A short reference following a piece of evidence, signaling to the reader that the information is not original to you as well as which source in your Works Cited this information came from. Every concrete detail, as long as it is not general knowledge, must be cited. The form that this reference takes depends on the style that your paper is written in.

Introduction: The first paragraph or section of an essay. Within this section, background information necessary to understand the essay itself is presented. The main topics of the essay are also mentioned here. The last sentence of the introduction paragraph/section is the thesis statement.

Thesis Statement: One sentence stating the main argument/theme of the paper. Thesis statements will also often include the main supporting arguments.

Topic Sentence: The first sentence of a body paragraph. A strong topic sentence includes the subject of the paragraph and how that topic relates to the thesis.

Works Cited: A section at the end of a paper, containing the full citations for every source used within the paper.

Box 0.1: A Basic Essay

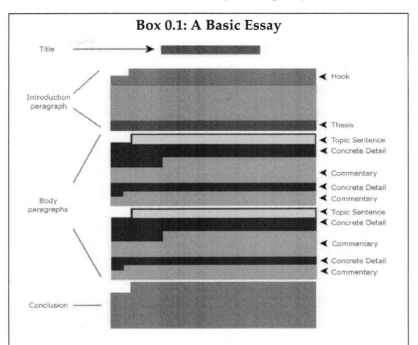

Box 0.1 Figure 0.1: Visual Diagram of a Basic Essay

Explanation: This is a good general example of an essay, but keep in mind that while most essays will be formatted like this, not all will. Most essays start with a title, centered at the top of the page. The first paragraph is the introduction, which commences with the hook and finishes with the thesis.

Next are the body paragraphs; there may be any number of body paragraphs, depending on the overall length of the essay. Each body paragraph starts with a topic sentence and includes both concrete detail and commentary. Concrete details are usually followed by commentary. Body paragraphs always end with commentary, not concrete details. The final paragraph in the essay is the conclusion.

Chapter 1: The Prompt

1. Read through the entire prompt, start to finish.

The most important part of starting a paper is that you understand what the prompt is asking. This might sound like very basic advice, but misinterpreting the prompt is a common problem. This can lead to two main issues: either not answering the entire question or becoming derailed and writing a paper that does not actually address the prompt, despite how thorough it may be. Of course, the product of both is the same—a poor grade.

Therefore, start off by carefully reading the prompt, even if you believe you already know what it is asking. Reading the prompt aloud will force you to slow down as you enunciate each word, allowing for better comprehension.

2. Now read through it again, underlining the important words or phrases.

Note the Number of Questions
Rarely does a prompt only focus on one topic; usually there are two or three main ideas that must be addressed.

Always remember that your professor will expect a cohesive, unified paper, so if the prompt is asking you to write about multiple ideas then they must be related in some way. As you underline the different ideas, think about how they are related and how you will connect them in your paper.

Determine the Length of the Sections

The length of the entire paper is often stated outright, but if your paper has multiple sections then the relative lengths of each section are usually left up to you to decide. The word "summarize" usually indicates that the section should be relatively short, while sections that ask you to explain, support an opinion or draw a conclusion will usually be longer. If two parts of the prompt are given equal emphasis, then their corresponding lengths in the essay should also be roughly equal. If you are unsure what the majority of the paper should focus on, then this is something to clarify with your instructor.

Note Any Quantity Words in the Prompt

Other key items to observe are any quantity words in your prompt. Are you being asked for a description of one event, several events, a series of events, or one main event? If the prompt mentions a specific number (i.e. one event, two memories, three articles) then that number is non-negotiable. Write any more or any less and you will not actually address the prompt fully and it will be impossible for most professors to give you a great grade, no matter how fantastic the rest of the essay may be.

For example, if the prompt asks for "several events," then the word "several" signifies between two and four. If the prompt asks for a "series of events," it is asking for three or more and the events must be related. Finally, if the prompt asks for one "main" or "primary" event, then the bulk of your paper should be focused on one topic in particular, but several other subjects can be mentioned (usually with the purpose of illuminating the primary focus).

Sometimes the prompt will not spell out the quantities in such direct terms, and here is where it is important to pay attention to words that are plural (have an "s" on the end), if there are any descriptors (such as "briefly" or "in detail"), or if your instructor gives any further direction when introducing the prompt.

Note Any Boundary Marker Words in the Prompt

The last point of a prompt you should pay attention to is the "boundary marker words." These words narrow the focus and define the boundaries for what an acceptable response can be. For example, if the prompt asks for you to discuss "*after* the climax of the book", then your focus should not be from *before* the climax. If the prompt asks you to talk about your childhood, then you should keep your response to the proper childhood years and not delve into your exciting job at a fish cannery after college. If the prompt asks you to focus on the main character, do not start talking about the sidekick unless it is to illustrate a quality of the primary character. Please refer to Box 1.1 for an example of decoding a prompt using these guidelines.

3. Identify what kind of essay your prompt is asking for.

In general, there are three main categories of essays: informative essays, persuasive essays and narrative essays. Informative essays deliver information about a topic without trying to convince the audience of anything. Persuasive essays state an opinion and support it with specific concrete details and commentary, trying to sway the readers to that point of view. Narrative essays tell a story, often about a personal experience.

Box 1.1: Decoding an Example Prompt

Example Prompt: Summarize the three short stories by Jack London that we read during class and then take a stance on the relationship between humans and nature.

Explanation: This prompt is asking you to do two things. First, the word "summarize" means that you need to give a brief summary of the three short stories (this signals to the professor that you read and understood them).

Second, "take a stance" means you must argue an opinion. The prompt specifies that your opinion must be about "the relationship between humans and nature." Unstated, though implied, is that you should support your opinion with concrete details from the three short stories, as the mention of the three short stories provides the set-up for the second part of the prompt.

Informative Essays

Informative essay prompts only ask for facts and do not ask you to argue any particular viewpoint (see Box 1.2). This essay is not about your opinion and should be as unbiased as possible.

Informative essays are distinct because your thesis will not state an opinion, but will merely provide a basic outline to let your audience know the direction of your paper. Instead of using commentary to persuade the audience, its purpose is to explain the concrete details and tie the facts together cohesively. Therefore, an informative essay will usually require less commentary and more concrete details than a persuasive essay.

Box 1.2: Example Informative Essay Prompts

Prompt 1: Explore the background of Jack London before he wrote "To Build a Fire." Did he have any training as a writer?

Prompt 2: The Yukon Gold Rush was a very important phenomenon in the late 19th century and it had many far-reaching impacts. Present the main positive and negative effects of the Gold Rush.

Explanation: Both of these informative essay prompts use detached words, such as "explore" and "present," to outline the essay requirements. Unlike opinionated words such as "argue," these words imply that a factual response is required.

The first prompt asks two questions and includes the clear boundary marker phrase "before he wrote 'To Build a Fire,'" defining the scope of the essay. The second prompt also wants you to discuss two areas: the positive and the negative effects of the Gold Rush. Neither aspect is emphasized more within the prompt, so the essay itself should be divided equally between the two topics.

Persuasive Essays

Persuasive essays are the most common type of writing prompt and there are many different varieties (see Box 1.3). In general, they will all be constructed the same way and they are all asking the same question—what is your stance on a topic and why? The thesis should clearly contain your argument or opinion and briefly list the main reasons supporting your stance. The bulk of this type of essay will be persuasive commentary, illustrating why your chosen concrete details support your opinion. The Example Throughout the Process essay for Chapters 1-8 is based on a persuasive essay prompt (see Box 1.4).

Box 1.3: Example Persuasive Essay Prompts

Prompt 1: In "To Build a Fire," pride is emphasized and plays an important role in the story. What do you think is a good definition of pride? Support your answer with quotes from the story.

Prompt 2: Give a short summary of "To Build a Fire." Did you find the story effective? Why or why not?

Explanation: The focus of both of these prompts is your opinion on a topic: your personal definition of pride and if the story was effective. Whenever you are asked for your opinion, you must provide strong support for your point of view; try to convince the audience that your opinion is right. Both prompts also require concrete details taken from "To Build a Fire." The first prompt directly states this, and the second implies it by first requiring a summary of the story. Providing strong concrete details will be vital in supporting your opinion, and each concrete detail must be accompanied by commentary to directly tie it to your main argument.

Box 1.4: Example Throughout the Process

Prompt: In the short story "To Build a Fire," what is the protagonist's fatal flaw that leads to his death? Why do you think so?

Explanation: I have selected a persuasive essay prompt for the Example Throughout the Process sections in Chapters 1-11. The skills needed in writing an informative essay are included, plus extra steps are taken to make the sample essay persuasive. The length of the final persuasive Example Throughout the Process paper is about 1500 words, or four double-spaced pages.

Looking at this prompt, I knew that it was asking for a persuasive essay, not an informative one, because the "fatal flaw" is not a cut-and-dried fact in the short story. The question "why do you think so" emphasized that I must argue *my* opinion. Continuing to decipher the prompt, the main phrase that jumped out at me was "the fatal flaw." "The" is singular, which told me that we were looking for one, and only one, reason behind the Man's death.

Next, I recognized a boundary marker phrase, "in the short story 'To Build a Fire,'" which signaled that the paper should be focused only on this short story. This meant that even if other stories by Jack London were read, even a prequel or sequel explaining back story on the Man, only information from this specific story could be used for my paper. Finally, I looked at the phrase "why do you think so." In addition to signaling that this was a persuasive essay, this phrase also acted as a red flag that the paper required in-depth explanation. For example, if my first instinct had been to write that the Man's fatal flaw was building his fire under a tree with snow on it, this additional question reminded me that I needed to push my explanation a bit further.

Narrative Essays

This type of essay is different from the other two in that the finished draft doesn't need to have a thesis, concrete details or commentary. The prompts for this type of essay will often specify that you must "tell a story" or "describe a scenario" (see Box 1.5). Because a narrative essay is so different in form, you cannot follow the same steps to write it as the other types of essays.

After decoding the prompt as described in this chapter, please refer to Chapter 2: Brainstorming, and then to Chapter 12: Narrative Essays for the next steps to answer this type of prompt. There is a separate Example Throughout the Process essay, based a narrative prompt (see Box 1.6), for Chapter 12.

Box 1.5: Example Narrative Essay Prompts

Prompt 1: In "To Build a Fire," the main character undergoes a conflict with an uncaring, impassive force: Nature. Reflect on a time when you had a similar conflict. What force were you conflicting with? How did you resolve it?

Prompt 2: Think of a time when you were terrified. Describe the event and your emotions during it, focusing on creating detailed descriptions.

Explanation: These prompts revolve around describing personal experiences; the responding essays will therefore read more like stories. The first prompt asks two distinct questions and limits the scope of the response to the type of conflict mentioned in the first sentence: a person conflicting with an uncaring, impassive force. While the prompt does not directly state that the "uncaring, impassive force" in your response should be nature, that

---

333333333

interpretation is hinted at in the first sentence. The second prompt only asks about one topic but emphasizes the importance of detailed descriptions, both for the event and for your emotions.

Box 1.6: Example Throughout the Process

Prompt: "To Build a Fire" depicts a conflict between Man and Nature. Using vivid sensory imagery, describe a time when you experienced a conflict with Nature. Was there a clear winner in the conflict?

Explanation: This is the prompt used in the Example Throughout the Process section for a narrative paper. This prompt is asking me to do two things: describe a conflict and say if there was a victor. Implied, though not stated outright, is the need to explain the answer to the second question—otherwise this would be a short answer question, not an essay prompt! The final draft of this example essay is around 750 words (a little over two pages, double spaced), but your assignment may be much longer.

Takeaway Points

- Understand what the prompt wants:
  - How many questions is the prompt asking?
  - How long should the paper or the sections in the paper be?
  - Are there any quantity words (words that specify a specific number of items) in the prompt?
  - Are there any boundary words (words that narrow the scope of an acceptable response) in the prompt?
  - What type of essay is the prompt asking for?

- Informative essays objectively tell the readers about a topic (your opinion should not be included).

- Persuasive essays argue to convince readers of your opinion.

- Narrative essays tell a story.

Chapter 2: Brainstorming

Brainstorming is the important process of collecting possible ideas to write about *before* the writing process begins. Rather than using the first idea you strike upon, brainstorming forces you to stop and think a bit more critically before starting your rough draft. This should give you several possible topics for your essay to focus on, allowing you to choose the best one for your response.

Even if you are absolutely positive that you know what you want to write about, a solid brainstorming session can be quite beneficial. For example, your brainstormed ideas may serve as inspiration for different parts of your response.

Before you can begin the brainstorming process, it is an excellent idea to re-read or skim over short stories or articles in order to refresh your memory. This is not yet the time to be looking for quotes or concrete details to use in your paper, but rather to ensure that you have a grasp of the main ideas.

1. Use at least one brainstorming technique.

The most important idea in brainstorming is not to get

stuck on one idea, but instead to explore several different facets responding to the prompt. Additionally, do not self-edit. During your brainstorming, try to think of a wide variety of possible responses without worrying about which would lead to the strongest paper. After the brainstorming session is complete, then you can start to sift through the ideas you have come up with.

There are several different brainstorming techniques that are common. It is up to you to try a few and decide which works best for you. Choose one and use it for at least ten minutes; this time span will give you enough time to delve beyond the ideas you may have already thought of.

Writing a List

Using a list for brainstorming means creating a bare-bones series of ideas and key words—these will not be in complete sentences (see Box 2.1).

Box 2.1: Example of Brainstorming by Writing a List

Prompt: What was the Man's fatal flaw?

Brainstorming List:
- Building his fire under a tree with snow
- Not bringing a companion with him
- Going out in the cold weather
- Why did he go out if it was so cold?
- Being cocky
- Not listening to advice of old men
- Not realizing that very cold weather could be dangerous
- Not understanding that building a fire under a tree could be bad
- He doesn't make the link between the risky conditions and the danger they mean

---

The benefit of a list is that you do not need to have any order to your ideas, so you can put them down quickly, plus lists are simple to make and to look at. However, a drawback is that it can be difficult to find organization or links among your ideas.

Visual Representations

Common visual representations for brainstorming include idea webs, Venn diagrams and T-charts. These are all similar ways of brainstorming and connecting information graphically. A benefit of these methods is that it is easy to see how the different ideas branch off of and relate to one another. The drawback is that visual representations can become quite complicated and are sometimes overwhelming.

An idea web begins by writing a key word or phrase from the prompt in the middle of a piece of paper. Next, add related ideas around this central phrase and draw lines linking the new ideas to the key word. If one of these ideas sparks a thought, write down your new ideas branching off of it. Ideas that are interconnected can also be connected with a line (see Box 2.2 Figure 2.1).

A Venn diagram begins by drawing two or more large circles on a piece of paper, slightly overlapping. Each circle stands for a topic and you can write brainstormed ideas relating to that individual topic within the circle. However, when an idea can be applied to multiple topics, it is placed within the overlapping space shared by those circles. This type of brainstorming can be especially useful for compare/contrast essays (see Box 2.3 Figure 2.2).

A T-chart is helpful when you are brainstorming

Box 2.2: Example of an Idea Web

Prompt: What was the Man's fatal flaw?

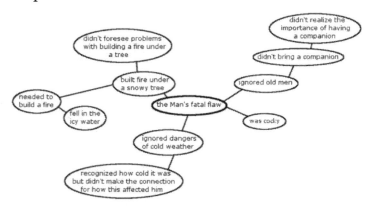

Box 2.2 Figure 2.1: Example of Idea Web Brainstorming

Explanation: This idea web started with the main part of the prompt, "the Man's fatal flaw." From there, I brainstormed several different topics branching out. One of these points, "fell in the icy water," eventually led back to one of the other topics, "built fire under a snowy tree." Some of the ideas didn't relate as well, such as "was cocky." When reviewing this idea web, three main conclusions jumped out as the strongest answers: "didn't foresee problems with building a fire under a tree," "recognized how cold it was but didn't make the connection for how this affected him" and "didn't realize the importance of having a companion."

for multiple topics or sides to a topic, such as for a compare/contrast essay or when the prompt addresses multiple points. Start by drawing a large capital "T" on a piece of paper. Each side of the vertical line represents a topic and is where you write the brainstormed points for that particular topic. After both sides have been brainstormed for, you can compare one side against the other to find points in common, areas that differ and overall trends.

Free Writing

If you find yourself hitting writer's block when beginning

Box 2.3: Example of Venn Diagram

Prompt: Compare and contrast the Man and the Dog in the short story "To Build a Fire."

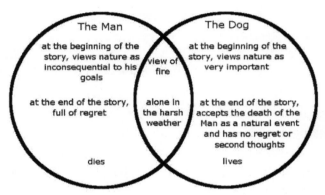

The Man — at the beginning of the story, views nature as inconsequential to his goals; at the end of the story, full of regret; dies

view of fire; alone in the harsh weather

The Dog — at the beginning of the story, views nature as very important; at the end of the story, accepts the death of the Man as a natural event and has no regret or second thoughts; lives

Box 2.3 Figure 2.2: Example of Venn Diagram Brainstorming

Explanation: Because this prompt asked for two items to be compared and contrasted, a Venn Diagram is a great visual brainstorming method to use. The two main subjects at hand, the Man and the Dog, are each written in one circle.

Points that are specific to each topic (that they do not share in common) are written in their respective circles. Aspects that the Man and the Dog have in common, such as their view of fire, are placed in the overlapping area to signal that they apply to both subjects. When reviewing this diagram, it's easy to see what these two subjects have in common and what is different between them.

---

a paper, then free writing is a great way to get ideas flowing. This technique is different from writing a list because you will be writing a stream of consciousness in paragraph form (see Box 2.4); you should literally write every thought going through your head.

Sometimes, when faced with a severe case of writer's block, I find it best to simply start writing with "I have no idea what to write for this prompt..." and by the time I've finished the sentence I am able to continue writing. Afterwards, simply sift the genuine ideas from the random thoughts.

Box 2.4: Example of Brainstorming by Free Writing

Prompt: What was the Man's fatal flaw?

Brainstorming Free Writing: "Alright, I am writing about what the fatal flaw of the Man was. Obviously, he ended up dead, and someone who was flawless would end up alive, so why did he die? He stepped in the cold water, which could be due to the flaw of not being cautious enough. He seemed fairly cautious though...

Obviously, it was bad that he didn't have a companion with him. Why did he make so many poor decisions? Did he not understand that going out in the cold, without a companion, and building a fire under a snow-laden tree would lead to trouble? Did he not see that he could die? Maybe he couldn't see that?"

Sifting Through the Free Write: When reviewing this free-write, I see several important points to include in my essay. First, I have a few examples that have sprung to mind concerning the Man and his flaws:
•Stepping in cold water
•Having no companion

> •Building a fire under a tree
> •Going out in such severe weather
> Second, I have linked many of these ideas together with one overarching theme: The Man did not make the connection that these events could lead to his death. This prominent point will become the main idea, or thesis, for my essay, while the other relevant points will form my support.

Discuss with a Friend

When the act of writing down your ideas is too intimidating or the words are not flowing, grab someone and start discussing the prompt. This person could be from your class or could be someone with no knowledge of your topic. Start off by simply discussing what the prompt is asking. What ideas spring to mind?

The idea is for your friend to nudge you for elaboration when you are on a roll or encourage you to talk your way through any block. An outside perspective also provides the benefit of new ideas and conclusions that you may not have reached on your own. This is an alternative to free writing, since free writing is, in essence, having a conversation with yourself. Often it is beneficial to follow this method up with one of the others, like making a list or a chart to consolidate and visualize your ideas.

2. Choose the focus of your paper.

Now that you have a variety of brainstormed ideas, go back to your prompt. What ideas best address the prompt? Automatically cross out anything that does not specifically answer the prompt or would need some twisting to directly relate. These will be difficult to work with and you will end up wrestling your commentary to show how they are directly relevant to the prompt.

If the prompt only asks one question, then once you have cut the options that don't answer the prompt, review the remaining possibilities. Is there an overarching idea that relates some, or all, of these points together? Does one point stand out as clearly stronger than the rest? It is this overarching idea or one strong point that will be the main focus of your paper and will form the backbone of your thesis. See Box 2.5 for a demonstration of this technique with the Example Throughout the Process.

If the prompt asks multiple questions, look at your brainstorming session(s). Which brainstormed ideas are best at answering each prompt question while working together to form a cohesive whole? In other words, find the concepts that best answer each question in the prompt and then try to find an idea or theme that they all share. This overarching theme will be the main focus of your paper, with your answer to each question forming the supporting subsections.

Regardless of how many questions there are in the prompt, once you finish brainstorming, the main focus of your paper should be clear and you should be able to write it out in one succinct phrase or sentence. If you are writing a persuasive essay, your opinion should come across easily in the main focus—after all, the purpose of a persuasive essay is to convey your opinion.

Box 2.5: Example Throughout the Process

Main Idea Developed in My Brainstorming Process: I think that the Man does not make the link between the risky conditions and the dangers presented to him, which is the fatal flaw that leads to his death.

Explanation: In my brainstorming sessions, I thought of several logical reasons for why the Man died. After narrowing down my ideas to the most important, I ended up with several strong possibilities. These ideas all related to the Man not making the link between danger and personal consequences, so I decided to make that the focus of my paper. This idea will be developed as the central argument and the thesis statement of the paper.

---

3. Brainstorm two to four supporting topics.

Once you have the main focus of your paper, turn your attention to how you will support this idea. Review the other points you have brainstormed. Which of these points support or funnel into your main focus?

You will need two to four supporting topics. You may need to do more brainstorming, if you do not have strong potential supporting topics in your previous brainstorming session. Think about why you chose your main focus as the best response to the prompt. What do you need to explain so the readers will have the same understanding that you do? These supporting topics will be developed into your body paragraphs (see Box 2.6 for the Example Throughout the Process).

Keep in mind that supporting topics are not concrete details (specific pieces of evidence, often facts, quotes or paraphrases) but instead are the most important ideas or reasons that reinforce and explain your main focus. For example, if my main focus is "winter is a better season than summer," a supporting topic might be "winter offers more sport possibilities than summer." This is not a concrete detail itself; it is my opinion and is not a specific fact. This supporting topic can be reinforced with concrete details. It is *not* possible for a supporting topic to be "68% of Americans play winter sports," as that statement is a concrete detail (a fact).

Do not worry about collecting a long list of concrete details now, because the thesis and supporting topics must first be shaped and put on paper. However, if several examples jump out at you then you should make a note of them. Often, this is a natural by-product of the

---

Box 2.6: Example Throughout the Process

Supporting Points Developed Through Brainstorming:
- The Man did not make the link between the intense cold and the danger to himself.
- The Man did not make the link between having a companion and possible benefits in the Yukon wilderness.
- The Man did not foresee problems with building a fire underneath a snow-filled tree.

Explanation: These three ideas were all present in my brainstorming session. Here, I made it clear that they supported the overarching idea of the Man not making the link between risky conditions and danger to himself.

Rather than being unrelated points, they clearly represent different facets of my main idea. They are effective supporting topics because they are precise (each covers a specific type of situation) without being facts and they work together to support the overall focus of the paper.

---

brainstorming process, so you may already have some concrete details in mind.

Remember, even if you are writing a long paper, you will still have only two to four supporting topics; the extra length will come from additional concrete details, commentary and possibly subdividing the supporting topics (where each supporting topic leads the readers through several closely-related points). Creating subsections is covered in Chapter 4, Step 7.

4. Create a rough outline.

You now have the main focus of your paper as well as two to four supporting topics. These will form the skeleton of your paper. For clarity, take the time now to write them in the form of an outline: the main focus first, followed by the supporting topics. Don't worry about having perfect word choice at this point in time. Refer to Box 2.7 for the rough outline of the Example Throughout the Process.

Box 2.7: Example Throughout the Process

Main Focus: I think that the Man does not make the link between the risky conditions and the dangers presented to him, which is the fatal flaw that leads to his death.

Supporting Topic 1: The Man did not make the link between the intense cold and the danger to himself.

Supporting Topic 2: The Man did not foresee problems with building a fire underneath a snow-filled tree.

Supporting Topic 3: The Man did not make the link between having a companion and possible benefits in the Yukon wilderness.

Explanation: Even though I only tweaked the wording,

---

writing a clear outline like this helped to cement the important points of my paper. I could clearly see the main focus and could check one more time that each supporting topic funneled back to the primary idea.

Takeaway Points

- The main brainstorming techniques include:
  - Writing a list
  - Using visual representations, such as idea webs
  - Free writing
  - Discussing with a friend

- Try not to self-edit while brainstorming.

- Every paper should have *one* main focus.

- Use the brainstorming session to choose *two* to *four* topics that support your main focus.

- Creating a rough outline is a good way to ensure the main focus and supporting topics are clear and related.

Chapter 3: Drafting the Thesis

1. Summarize the main idea of your essay in one sentence.

Being on the right track with the focus of your essay at this point can mean the difference between a writing process that is straight-forward and organized, or one that is confusing and lengthy. The thesis is the main foundation of the drafting process, and should feature either an opinion or a central topic.

Think of writing a paper as having a conversation. If the prompt is simply a question posed to you, then the thesis is the short version of your answer. Unless you are specifically instructed otherwise, all informative and persuasive papers must include a clearly stated thesis in the final draft.

Informative essays do not argue an opinion, so the purpose of the thesis is simply to explain the main theme that the essay will focus on. In a persuasive essay, the most important aspect is your stance. It is vital that your main theme or opinion is clearly stated in the first draft of your thesis, as it will ease the creation of the body of your essay.

Look at the primary idea you brainstormed in

Section 3 of the previous chapter and write it as a complete sentence, thinking of it as a strong, one-sentence response to the prompt. Make sure this sentence directly responds to all parts (or the most important parts) of the prompt. This is the rough draft of your thesis.

2. Avoid merely restating the prompt.

Does your thesis simply restate the question presented in the prompt? It is vital to have a thesis that brings in new information or opinions and clearly *answers* the prompt. The clearer the thesis is, the easier it will be to construct a high quality paper. It is important that you include a specific topic (informative essay) or an opinion (persuasive essay) and don't merely rephrase the prompt (see Box 3.1).

Box 3.1: Ineffective and Effective Theses Examples

Sample Prompt: Compare and contrast the Man and the Dog in the short story, "To Build a Fire."

Ineffective Thesis Statement: The Man and the Dog had many similarities and differences.
Explanation: This thesis does not express any opinion and merely restates the prompt.

Ineffective Thesis Statement: The Man and the Dog differ in their regard of nature at the beginning of the short story "To Build a Fire."
Explanation: The prompt asked for two items of equal weight: compare and contrast. This sentence, however, only mentions the contrast between the Man and the Dog. Because both items are equally significant in the prompt, both must be represented in the thesis for it to be a full response to the prompt.

> **Effective Thesis Statement:** The Man and the Dog differ in their regard of nature at the beginning of the short story "To Build a Fire," but are similar in their regard of fire throughout the story.
> **Explanation:** This thesis is the strongest because it responds to the entire prompt and answers the implied question: *"How* are the Man and the Dog similar or different?"* This thesis adds additional information and opinions (because the prompt is for a persuasive essay) rather than merely rephrasing the prompt.

3. Add a "because" phrase to your thesis.

At this point, you have written the main part of your thesis, either your opinion or the theme of the paper. However, the thesis is also usually used to introduce the supporting points. After reading your thesis, readers will be able to better orient themselves within your essay and will have a clearer understanding of the progression of your ideas.

A common form for a Persuasive Essay thesis is:

I believe in X because of A, B and C.

While a common form for an Informative Essay thesis is:

My topic is X in terms of A, B and C.

The phrases "I believe in X" and "My topic is X" are your main opinion or theme, while "A," "B" and "C" represent the two to four main supporting topics listed in your outline.

Remember, you have already written the first part of your thesis ("I believe in X" or "my topic is X") in the first thesis rough draft. Now you have to fill in the rest, a summary of each of your supporting topics ("because of/in terms of A, B and C"). You have already written these ideas out as general points in the outline you created in the previous chapter, but now you need to find a way to summarize these topics into a word or a short phrase. Creating a shorter version of your supporting topics will make them easier to integrate into your thesis statement as the "A, B and C" portion. See Box 3.2 for the Example Throughout the Process of this step.

As you are creating this draft of the thesis, keep in mind the idea of parallel structure for your supporting topics. This means that each item in your list should be written in a comparable way. For example, if one of your supporting topics is summarized as one word, and one is summarized as a long phrase, it will feel uneven. Your thesis will sound much smoother if each item in the list is a similar length and follows a similar structure (see Box 3.3).

Box 3.2: Example Throughout the Process

Supporting Topic 1: The Man did not make the link between the intense cold and the danger to himself.
Summary of Topic 1: Elemental hazards
Explanation for Topic 1: This topic could be summarized as "cold temperature" or "elemental hazards." I chose to use "elemental hazards" for my thesis because I wanted to emphasize the danger aspect and the weather as a whole.

Supporting Topic 2: The Man did not think about potential issues of building a fire underneath a snow-filled tree.
Summary of Topic 2: Failure to build a fire.
Explanation for Topic 2: I chose the most important result,

"failure to build a fire," rather than addressing a cause (the location under a snow-filled tree). While it was tempting to summarize this topic as "not being able to build a fire," it flowed better to use a positive statement rather than a negative one (negative statements use "not").

Supporting Topic 3: The Man did not make the link between the benefits of having a companion and its critical importance in the Yukon wilderness.
Summary of Topic 3: Traveling alone.
Explanation for Topic 3: Initially I wanted to summarize this as "not having a companion." However, just as I chose to use a positive statement with Supporting Topic 2, it was also better to use a positive statement here.

Working Thesis: I believe the Man's fatal flaw is his inability to understand the effects of his own decisions, including *his lack of appreciation of elemental hazards, his failure to build fire and his insistence on traveling alone.*

Explanation: As I added these topics into the thesis, I rephrased them a bit so the list would sound smoother and would clearly support my main argument. I also made each item in the list of supporting topics have a similar grammatical structure so they would be parallel with each other. Each item starts with "his _____."

By starting this way, with a noun at the beginning of each item, the items in the list are parallel and immediately sound much more polished. This thesis still needs some revising, but already clearly contains all the main points and is a manageable length.

Box 3.3: Parallel Structure Examples

Example of a list without parallel structure: I like skiing, books and to watch movies.

Example of a list with parallel structure: I like skiing, reading books and watching movies.

Explanation: The first list starts with a verb in the "-ing" form ("skiing"), then lists a noun ("books") and finishes with a verb in the infinitive form ("to watch"). The second example is much more successful because each item in the list starts with a verb in the "-ing" form ("skiing," "reading" and "watching").

---

4. Use specific word choice.

Especially when you are writing your thesis, avoid using the first person (I, me, we, us, our), as it is considered vague, informal and not appropriate for academic writing. When reading an academic paper, the audience understands that all the opinions expressed are yours, so it is not necessary to write "I believe."

If your paper is about a particular story, article, film or other work, it is vital that the name of the work and the creator's name (author, director, etc.) are included in the thesis. If your paper is focused around a specific character, include either the name or the type of character (such as "protagonist" or "antagonist"), whichever would be clearer. Think of the thesis as a self-contained idea. It should be able to be removed from your paper and it will still contain all the important information needed to understand your topic or argument. See Box 3.4 for refining the Example Throughout the Process thesis.

Box 3.4: Example Throughout the Process

Thesis Draft: I believe the Man's fatal flaw is his inability to understand the effects of his own decisions, including his lack of appreciation of elemental hazards, his failure to build fire and his insistence on traveling alone.

Revised Thesis: *Jack London's "To Build a Fire" presents the protagonist's final downfall as his failure to assess the repercussions of his own decisions,* including his lack of appreciation of elemental hazards, his failure to build fire and his insistence on traveling alone.

Explanation: At this stage, I have refined the thesis draft into a stronger, more specific thesis statement. I removed the first person "I think..." and added the name and author of the story. Clarity was improved by adding proper nouns, including replacing "the Man," which could be confusing, with "the protagonist." I rephrased "inability to understand the effects" to "failure to assess the repercussions," which is more specific. This thesis is strong because it clearly answers the prompt, it presents the main points the essay will cover, it includes the title of the story and the author's name and it uses specific wording.

---

5. Create a revised outline.

Now that you have the final draft of your thesis, let's revisit the outline you created in Section 5 of Chapter 2. Place the polished thesis statement at the top of the outline. Below it, list your two to four main topics of support. Use this time to revise the word choice of the main topics of support, making sure they support the new thesis without directly repeating any phrases. The revised Example Throughout the Process outline can be found in Box 3.5.

Box 3.5: Example Throughout the Process

Thesis: Jack London's "To Build a Fire" presents the protagonist's final downfall as his failure to assess the repercussions of his own decisions, including his lack of appreciation of elemental hazards, his failure to build fire and his insistence on traveling alone.

Supporting Topic 1: The Man did not make the link between the intense cold and the danger to himself.

Supporting Topic 2: The Man did not think about potential issues of building a fire underneath a snow-filled tree.

Supporting Topic 3: The Man did not make the link between the benefits of having a companion and its critical importance in the Yukon wilderness.

Takeaway Points

• A strong thesis does *not* simply restate the prompt.

• A strong thesis *does*: represent the focus of your essay, have a "because" phrase mentioning your supporting topics and use detailed word choice.

• Having a clear outline of the body of your essay is a vital backbone to drafting your thesis.

• A complete, quality outline includes: a specific thesis statement and simple, clear, related supporting topics.

Chapter 4: Concrete Details

At this point in time, you should have a solid version of your thesis. You should also have two to four supporting topics, which back up and elaborate on your thesis. Now it is time to collect concrete details, which include facts, quotes, summaries and paraphrases. You must provide a sufficient number of concrete details to back up each of your supporting topics.

Think of your essay like a pyramid, with the foundation formed from solid, inarguable concrete details. These concrete details provide the foundation for your supporting topics, which in turn lead to your thesis—the pinnacle of the pyramid and of your paper (see Box 4.1 Figure 4.1).

As you collect your concrete details, remember that your final draft must include a citation, or reference to its source, for each one or it will be considered plagiarism. Citations tell the readers where the concrete details came from. As you collect your concrete details, note where you found them with page numbers, book titles, article titles and/or web addresses. We will address writing complete citations in Chapter 9.

Box 4.1: Concrete Detail Foundation

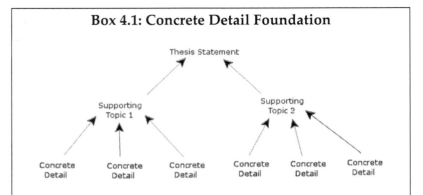

Box 4.1 Figure 4.1: Visual Diagram of Concrete Detail Foundation

Explanation: The concrete details provide a sturdy foundation for the entire paper. They reinforce the supporting topics and everything works together to uphold the thesis.

1. Gather a variety of resources.

The word "resources" refers to the sources of support you will use in your essay. You may only need one resource or you may need to find many. For example, if you are writing an analysis of a book then you will only need the book itself, whereas if you are writing a lengthy research paper then you may need many resources.

Books

Books are a traditional, tried-and-true resource. They are useful because their information is usually verified and they provide a clear context.

One drawback to using books as resources is that they usually do not contain extremely current information, due to the turnaround time for publishing. This may not be critical for a literary analysis or a historical essay, but it can be debilitating if you are writing a paper about a new scientific method or a recent psychological theorem.

Journal Articles

A journal article is a peer-reviewed article appearing in an academic publication, a periodical which is usually released multiple times a year. Journal articles may appear intimidating to students who have not used them before, but they are often very accessible, quick to read and full of up-to-date information.

Often, these articles can be found in online databases (such as *Jstor* or *ScienceDirect*), which are available with a subscription. Subscriptions are available to Universities, libraries, businesses or individuals, and many Universities provide membership to students, free of charge. There are also entirely free ways to view journal articles. "GoogleScholar" is a free search engine which searches through a variety of online databases, many of which allow you to read journal articles for free.

If you are new to using journal articles as a resource, the best way to start is by searching an online database. This method is fairly quick and easy, and can provide invaluable information. Prestigious journals require their articles to be peer-reviewed, which means that the articles' information must be evaluated by a group of professionals in the discipline to ensure that it is factually accurate.

Journal articles can be quite current; they present new information and ideas researched with the latest technology, which makes them a vital resource if your paper is on a contemporary topic. The primary drawback of using journal articles is gaining access to the articles you need. Many journal articles require a paid subscription to access and if you do not have a subscription then it can be costly or time-consuming to find their full text.

Video Resources

Video resources are generally used less often than print resources, but they can provide a fuller experience of a scene or time period. Video resources include documentaries, news clips, popular movies, independent movies and television broadcasts. You can use video resources to provide information, relate to your audience, or as the basis of analysis.

However, videos are often difficult to include as concrete details in your writing because you must precisely describe, without personal bias, the events on screen. Also, videos usually have a strong point of view and you will have to evaluate the accuracy and legitimacy of the information.

Newspapers

Newspapers are useful for researching current events, as well as providing concrete details for historical events. Past newspaper articles can be found at libraries or online. However, keep note that articles may be different between online and print versions and some information may be found in one but not the other.

When referencing newspaper articles, the main point to be wary of is the blurred lines between fact, conjecture and opinion. If you are writing a fact-driven paper, do not use newspapers as your sole resource. Pair the facts from the newspapers with facts from other, more reliable sources, such as journal articles or books, to yield a stronger basis of support.

Magazines

Both current and back issues of magazines can be found at libraries. This resource is useful if you are appealing to your reader or analyzing a popular culture phenomenon. A less common use is as a primary historical source. Many libraries keep much older magazines but you may have to ask to see them, as they are often kept in an archive. When you are using magazines as a resource, realize that the level of fact-checking can be extremely variable and the information in many magazines is not always considered reliable.

Websites

The Internet is the first choice resource of many students. While internet resources can be invaluable, it is necessary to be extra aware of each website's credibility as a source. Useful websites include often-updated reputable websites (such as government websites or international news organizations) and websites with online-specific information. Websites also do not usually provide the same level of depth or context as books or journals.

Wikipedia, even though it is an easy-to-use resource, is not viewed as a credible source by most teachers or professors. Almost anyone can edit or change most articles on Wikipedia. However, Wikipedia is useful for gaining a general understanding of your topic, before you find your concrete details in other, more credible, sources. If you aren't sure how to start finding more reliable sources, consider looking at the references at the bottom of most Wikipedia articles as a starting point.

Interviews

Interviews are particularly useful as firsthand accounts or opinions on a particular subject. If you intend to conduct an interview, learn if your professor has specific requirements for the interview process itself. For example, interviewees may need to sign a release to be quoted.

For formal interviews, the questions may need to be approved by an Institutional Review Board at your University and the interview itself may need to be audio-recorded, with the audio-recording saved for a certain amount of time. Even if it is not required, audio-recording an interview can be helpful by enabling you to focus on your subject. This avoids frantic note-taking during the conversation and allows you to refer back to the dialogue at your leisure.

Interviews can be conducted over the phone, face-to-face, or through writing. Brainstorm a list of questions you would like to ask during the interview and focus on how these questions will help further your thesis. However, don't be afraid to improvise if your interview subject mentions something related that you hadn't thought of.

When your interview is completed, transcribe the interview immediately. In your paper you may want to describe the scene or the tone of the interview and it is best to record those details while they are still fresh in your mind.

While useful for collecting firsthand accounts about a subject, interviews are subject to a host of drawbacks. The information presented may not be factually correct, the quality and quantity of concrete details you record will be dependent on your skills as an interviewer and an objective point of view may be almost impossible to find.

2. Know the types of concrete details.

Facts

Facts include statistics, dates and statements of events. A fact is a proven piece of evidence that cannot be argued (see Box 4.2). Facts are most effective when they are as specific as possible. An opinion should not be presented as a fact, whether it is yours or someone else's.

Box 4.2: Example Facts

Weak Fact: Studies show that more people enjoy warm weather than freezing temperatures.

Strong Fact: A 2005 study showed that 67% of people enjoy warm weather, while only 33% of people enjoy freezing temperatures.

Explanation: Both of these statements are facts, but the second includes more specific information and is therefore a stronger concrete detail. Stronger concrete details will be more convincing to your readers, will provide better support for your thesis and will be easier to write non-repetitive commentary for.

Quotes

A quote is an exact re-statement from the source material. When you include a quote in your paper, it must be surrounded by quotation marks and the quote must be a word-for-word replica of the original. If you want to remove part of the original quote, use an ellipsis ("...") to signal that part of the original text is missing. However, the overall meaning and tone of the original text must be kept intact. If there is a typo or grammatical error in the original text, place "[*sic*]" after the error to let your readers know that your quote is accurate and the error is from the original text (see Box 4.3).

Box 4.3: Example Shortened Quote with Original Error

Quote: In the article, Smith stated "the Nroth [*sic*] is a harsh…world" (129).

Explanation: In the original source material, the word "North" was misspelled. Because a quote must exactly restate the source material, the misspelling must be kept intact. However, adding [*sic*] lets your readers know that the misspelling is not a typo that you made. Here, the ellipsis is used to show that part of the original text, between "harsh" and "world," was taken out.

Quotes are best used when the exact wording of the source material is important, or when you cannot re-word or summarize it in an effective way. There are two ways to present quotations in your paper: integrated quotations and block quotations. Integrated quotations are short, usually one sentence or shorter, and are worked ("integrated") into the main text of your paper (see Box 4.4). Always try to make an integrated quote as short as you can without losing its meaning.

A block quotation is bigger than an integrated quote, usually four lines or longer, and is set apart in its own paragraph without quotation marks (see Box 4.5). Block quotations should be used when reading the entire quote is necessary for comprehension. However, try to

---

Box 4.4: Example Integrated Quotation

Integrated Quotation: The Man thought to himself, "Any man who was a man could travel alone" (London).

Explanation: This entire sentence is a concrete detail, with the first part giving the unbiased context of the quote. Using integrated quotes gives you the opportunity to smoothly include important information for the readers, such as who is speaking, when the quote occurs or who the quote is intended for.

---

limit their length and avoid having more than two block quotations per ten pages. Be wary of including block quotations when they are not completely necessary, as they may interrupt the flow of your paper and can feel unwieldy. Whenever possible, avoid block quotations and use one or more integrated quotations or paraphrases, as this will flow better for the readers and makes it easier to write commentary about the quotes themselves.

Summaries

A summary is a shorter, simplified version of an original text. The main ideas should be preserved but details will most likely be lost. In formal papers, summaries should usually be a maximum of five sentences and will often be even shorter. Be wary: summaries can easily become vague and too long, taking over your paper. Summaries work best as concrete details when referring to scientific journal articles, technical studies or specific case-studies, as the summaries of these would still convey specific, conclusive details. For most other works, summaries are best used in the introduction paragraph, the conclusion paragraph or when providing important context.

Box 4.5: Example of a Block Quotation

Block Quotation: The Man continues to deny his mistakes, despite mounting evidence:

> Those old-timers were rather womanish, some of them, he thought. All a man had to do was to keep his head, and he was all right. Any man who was a man could travel alone. But it was surprising, the rapidity with which his cheeks and nose were freezing. And he had not thought his fingers could go lifeless in so short a time. (London)

The Man is already brought face-to-face with several consequences from his decisions, including his cheeks, nose and fingers freezing.

Explanation: This block quotation is introduced by a sentence in my own words followed by a colon. The block quotation is easy to differentiate from the rest of the text because it is indented more.

   I might choose to use this block quote if the entire passage was important as a whole; for example, the entire quote would be needed if I wanted to talk about the quick change in tone from "mocking" in the first sentence to "surprised" in the last two sentences. This point could be best argued by including the entire passage, rather than picking out only a few quotes which might not convey the entire idea.

   After the block quotation, I have continued the paragraph in my own words. No additional indenting is needed here, because I am continuing the same paragraph.

Paraphrases

Paraphrasing is when you use your own words to express a phrase or passage from an outside source (see Box 4.6). A paraphrase should be about the same length as the source material and should faithfully represent the intent of the original text. This technique is often used when the original words were not incredibly compelling, when the original source was confusing or when a quote would be awkward to integrate into your paper. Paraphrasing allows you the opportunity to state the main ideas and relevant details in a source, while avoiding points that may be off-topic for your paper.

Box 4.6: Example of a Paraphrase

Original Quote: "When he fell down a second time, it [the Dog]...sat in front of him facing him curiously eager and intent. The warmth and security of the animal angered him, and he cursed it..." (London)

Paraphrase: After falling again, the Man feels anger towards the Dog for its animated and worry-free attitude. The Man curses the Dog, due to its safety and heat (London).

Explanation: This paraphrase is about the same length as the original and conveys the same ideas without putting words in the author's mouth or changing any original intent. I might choose to use a paraphrase instead of a quote for a few reasons.

First, the original quote uses all pronouns ("he" and "it" in the quote) and it might feel awkward in my text to explain or add in the names ("the Man" and "the Dog").

Second, two ellipses are used in the original quote. Ellipses are acceptable to use in quotes when you want to

---

> skip over some of the original text, but this may interrupt the flow of my paragraph.
>
> Third, the quote is written in the past tense, while literary papers usually describe literature in the present tense. Switching back and forth between the tenses here may be confusing or awkward-sounding.

3. List possible concrete details.

As you start your collection of concrete details, remember that you are finding evidence to reinforce your two to four supporting topics. Look for details that fall within those topics. Remember the pyramid structure of your paper—the concrete details should uphold your supporting topics and these supporting topics will funnel into your thesis.

Additionally, when you are collecting concrete details, remember that they should be as specific as possible. Do not take up time recording whole paragraphs; merely write the most important quote, fact or idea, and make a note of why you chose it and where it can be found. Organize your list of concrete details by which supporting point they uphold. This will make using your concrete details much easier as you assemble your essay.

While you are collecting this information, you may come across strong pieces of evidence revolving about a new supporting point you had not previously brainstormed. If this new supporting point adds a unique idea that concisely supports your thesis, it would be a good idea to write down this new topic and collect these concrete details. Try to avoid creating many new supporting topics, however, as this will be distracting and may lead to disorganization and a lack of focus. You will end up only using two to four supporting topics, so any surplus supporting topics will have to be culled before you start writing the paper itself.

Don't worry about the order of concrete details at this point! The pieces of evidence only need to be organized by the supporting topics, and any further organization will come later.

4. Collect more concrete details.

While searching for concrete details, it is always a good idea to find more than you think you might need. This allows you to pick the best support for your paper, which will not only make your paper stronger but will make your job of writing commentary much easier. It is important to have a strong, manageable amount of concrete details that are closely related to your thesis. Additionally, try to collect a similar amount of concrete details for each supporting point. In your essay, each supporting point should be similar in length and strength and you can start working towards this goal now.

When deciding how many concrete details you must find, keep in mind that generally a persuasive paper has about one concrete detail per two or three pieces of commentary, while an informative paper may have the opposite—two concrete details per one or two pieces of commentary.

5. Check that you have basic citations.

Before you go any further, make sure that you've collected the basic citation information for all of your concrete details and sources. Remember that a citation signals that the information is not your original idea and tells the audience where the information came from. The only time you do not need to include citations for concrete details is when the information is general knowledge, such as the year that World War II started or the capital of France.

Do not get caught up in writing full citations right now—after all, you don't even know if you will be using all of these concrete details! For now, just make sure you the author, title of the work, the page numbers and/or the web address. Double-checking that you have this information now will save you the work of having to re-find your sources again later.

6. Evaluate the spread of your concrete details.

At this point, you should have a decent number of concrete details (facts, quotes, summaries and/or paraphrases). Each of these should have a note of where you found the information, so you will be able to write citations for the sources you use in the final draft. Now it is time to evaluate how widely spread your concrete details are.

Look at the number of sources you are using. Remember, a source is where your concrete details are coming from. Your sources might be books, websites, videos, etc. You may be instructed to use a certain number of sources, but if it is unclear then just remember that the more varied your sources, the better supported your argument will be. It is much easier to find additional sources now then it will be later in the writing process! Not only should you have a variety of sources in your entire paper, but each supporting topic should have concrete details drawn from an array of sources.

If you are using only one source for your paper, then it is important that your evidence comes from different locations in that source. For example, rather than having three quotes from the same chapter, use one quote from the beginning of the book, one from the middle and one from the end. This shows that your argument has a wide, strong basis of support, rather than being built upon a small, potentially unsteady foundation. To review some of the concrete details collected for the Example Throughout the Process, refer to Box 4.7.

Box 4.7: Example Throughout the Process

In this section, I have included a partial list of the concrete details that I collected for my example paper. Each concrete detail is followed by a short explanation of why I chose it. For the complete list of concrete details I compiled for this step, please view Appendix IV.

Thesis: Jack London's "To Build a Fire" presents the protagonist's final downfall as his failure to assess the repercussions of his own decisions, including his lack of appreciation of elemental hazards, his failure to build fire and his insistence on traveling alone.

Concrete Detail 1: "Fifty degrees below zero was to him just precisely fifty degrees below zero. That there should be anything more to it than that was a thought that never entered his head" (London).

Explanation: I thought this was an interesting quote about the environmental hazards, where the Man did not speculate on the importance of the temperature—the thought never even entered his mind. This lack of foresight caught my attention as I re-read the story.

Concrete Detail 2: He "was astonished at the swift numbness that smote them"—referring to the Man's fingers after they had been out of their gloves for less than a minute (London).

Explanation: This is another concrete detail related to the cold temperature. I thought the use of the word "astonished" here was interesting, as it implies something that is unexpected. Despite having access to information about the temperature before leaving town, it appears that the Man did not extrapolate that knowledge out to how it would apply to him.

I also liked this quote because it emphasizes for the readers the coldness of the atmosphere and the gravity of the situation. Note that I included a phrase explaining the context of the quote. This is not a polished phrase or sentence at this point, but will be useful in reminding myself about this quote later in the writing process.

Concrete Detail 3: He knew the importance of preventing the flame from being drowned in snow—this is why he laid down the larger sticks over which he made his first fire (London).

Explanation: This is a paraphrase of the passage: "He threw down several large pieces on top of the snow. This served for a foundation and prevented the young flame from drowning itself in the snow it otherwise would melt" (London). I found this part of the story to be significant because it shows that the Man is not making these mistakes because he is inexperienced or ignorant.

7. Create subsections, if needed.

If you are writing a longer paper, you may need additional organization for the concrete details within each supporting topic. The process of subdivision takes the concrete details you have collected for each

70

supporting topic and groups them into subtopics. This will help your flow of ideas seem smoother and will aid the audience in following your argument.

For example, if the Example Throughout the Process essay was meant to be six thousand words instead of fifteen hundred, I would have collected many more concrete details for each supporting topic. If not subdivided, these concrete details would appear as a chaotic mass in each supporting topic. Subdividing each topic into several smaller groupings would help to maintain a clear flow of information.

With subdivision, if my first topic was "temperature," I would present multiple facets of this topic, such as "temperature before the Man leaves the village," "temperature as the Man is dying," and "temperature as perceived by the Dog." All three of these facets directly relate to the overall heading, "temperature," and in addition they each provide a different focus that supports both the topic sentence and the thesis (see Box 4.8).

Just as you are striving for each supporting topic to be of similar length and strength, if you choose to subdivide your supporting topics then these subdivisions must also feel balanced. The flow of a paper would most likely feel uneven if one supporting topic was subdivided into eight equally small sections, the next supporting topic was subdivided into two large sections and the final supporting topic was subdivided into one large section and three small sections. This would feel unbalanced and would be confusing to your readers. Each supporting topic should have a similar number of subdivisions and these subdivisions should be comparable in length.

Box 4.8: Example Outline of an Essay with Subdividing

Thesis: Jack London's "To Build a Fire" presents the protagonist's final downfall as his failure to assess the repercussions of his own decisions, including his lack of appreciation of elemental hazards, his failure to build fire and his insistence on traveling alone.

Supporting Topic 1: Elemental hazards

> **Subtopic 1:** Perception of cold temperatures at the beginning of the Man's trip
>
> **Subtopic 2:** Perception of cold temperatures after falling in the icy water

Supporting Topic 2: Inability to build a fire

> **Subtopic 1:** Knowledge in how to build a fire (both first and second fires) contrasted with avoidable mistakes due to lack of foresight
>
> **Subtopic 2:** Thought process after the failure of the second fire

Supporting Topic 3: Lack of a companion

> **Subtopic 1:** Views on having a companion just after starting his journey and experiencing the cold
>
> **Subtopic 2:** Refusal to take responsibility for choosing to not have a companion as the Man is dying

Explanation: If the Example Throughout the Process essay was significantly longer, this could be its outline with subdivided supporting topics. Each supporting topic has the same number of subdivisions (two) and, when written out, each subtopic paragraph would be of a similar length. The subdivisions for each supporting topic are unique aspects of that topic. For example, the first supporting topic is "elemental hazards." Both of the subtopics for that topic revolve around the harshness of the environment and challenges that the Man faces.

The subtopics have also been organized in the order that is most logical under each topic. Often, this is chronologically; for example, Supporting Topic 1 starts with the subtopic pertaining to the beginning of the trip, followed by the subtopic about the middle of the trip. Most importantly, always remember that subtopics always directly support the thesis.

If your paper will be long enough to warrant subsections, organize them now. Read through the concrete details you have found and look for common themes within the pieces of evidence for each supporting topic. What are some ways to organize the information under each topic? Remember that you have collected more concrete details than you will use, so right now you do not need exactly the same amount of concrete details in each subsection. In the next chapter, you will narrow down your concrete details to the strongest ones; at that step you will have the chance to ensure the subsections are equally weighted.

Takeaway Points

- There are many types of resources. Use the ones that are best for your type of paper:
  - **Books**: Have verified, comprehensive information. However, information may be out-of-date.
  - **Journals**: Have verified, current information. May be difficult or costly to access.
  - **Videos**: Give a full experience of a scene. May be difficult to describe without bias.
  - **Newspapers**: Useful when researching current or historical events. Must differentiate fact, conjecture and opinion.
  - **Magazines**: Useful for researching popular culture. Not factually reliable.
  - **Websites**: Easy to use and contain frequently-updated information. Reliability of information is extremely variable.
  - **Interviews**: Valuable source of first-person experiences. Difficult to evaluate reliability of facts and strength of bias.

- There are four main categories of concrete details: facts, quotes, summaries and paraphrases.

- Collecting a wide variety of concrete details will lead to a strong essay foundation.

- Don't forget to note where each piece of information came from, so that it will be easy for you to cite it!

- If your essay is long, subdivide each supporting topic for a clearer sense of organization.

Chapter 5: Commentary

1. Determine the ratio of concrete details to commentary.

The bulk of your paper will be your concrete details and commentary. Remember that concrete details are the quotes, paraphrases, facts and summaries that you have collected—the outside information that supports the thesis. On the other hand, commentary is where your voice can really shine. Commentary is used to explain the concrete details, to present your opinions and to clearly show the relation between the concrete details and thesis. Commentary usually does not need to be cited because all of the ideas should be original to you.

While commentary in all papers has a similar purpose, various types of papers require different amounts of commentary. In this step, you must decide on the ratio of concrete details to commentary based on the type of paper you are writing.

Informative Essay

Informative essays simply relate information without trying to persuade the audience to any one point of view. Because you are not giving your opinion, commentary plays a much smaller role; in this type of paper, commentary is generally used to clarify facts and provide a clear flow from one concrete detail to another. The emphasis here is on the concrete details. On average, there is one piece of commentary per two concrete details. Occasionally you may need more commentary if a concrete detail is confusing or if the relevance needs to be emphasized.

Persuasive Essay

The purpose of a persuasive essay is to convince the audience of a certain point of view through the use of effective commentary. Therefore, the ratio of commentary to concrete details is reversed from that of an informative essay. For persuasive essays, a good average is two to three sentences of commentary for every concrete detail.

Avoid listing multiple concrete details and then writing a block of commentary. It is much more effective to read one concrete detail, then read the related commentary sentences, then continue to the next concrete detail. This will help convince your audience by relating each concrete detail to your thesis and providing a smooth flow from one idea to the next.

2. Narrow the concrete details to a suitable amount.

As you gathered concrete details in Chapter 4, you focused on finding a surplus so you could choose the strongest for your paper. Now that you have established the ratio of concrete details to commentary needed for your paper, you can predict how many concrete details you should keep based on the essay's final length. One page of an informative essay will require more concrete details than a page of a persuasive essay.

As you select which concrete details to keep, remember the idea of keeping information from a variety of locations. Try to retain evidence from several different sources, or choose concrete details from throughout a single source (for example, avoid choosing three concrete details from the same page). Avoid repetitive concrete details—if you have multiple that demonstrate the exact same idea, or even a very similar concept, keep only the strongest.

Finally, remember to refer back to your thesis and choose the concrete details that provide the most direct support. As you read each concrete detail, ask yourself how it helps prove your thesis. Right now, go through your concrete details and keep only the best. For an example of this method, see the Example Throughout the Process in Box 5.1.

Box 5.1: Example Throughout the Process

To demonstrate, I narrowed down the concrete details I collected for my supporting topic "Environmental Hazards." From the initial seven concrete details, I chose the three strongest.

Keep: "Fifty degrees below zero was to him just precisely fifty degrees below zero. That there should be anything more to it than that was a thought that never entered his head."

Delete: "Fifty degrees below zero meant eighty odd degrees of frost. Such fact impressed him as being cold and uncomfortable, and that was all."

Explanation: These first two concrete details have very

---

similar ideas and both come from the beginning of the story. The first is stronger for my paper, because it emphasizes the Man's lack of foresight—the focus of my thesis.

Keep: When he spat, "There was a sharp, explosive crackle that startled him" but he did not think any more of it.
Explanation: The imagery and strong word choice, or diction, in the quote gives strong support for my thesis.

Delete: "He was surprised, however, at the cold."
Explanation: This concrete detail is weak because it doesn't bring in any new information, nor is it particularly memorable. The idea of the Man being surprised at the cold had already been addressed in the previous concrete detail and the word "cold" doesn't evoke any strong emotions or images.

Delete: "muzzle of ice"—the description of what chewing tobacco caused around his mouth. This "muzzle" held the Man's mouth closed, but he still continued chewing the tobacco.
Explanation: While I liked the image of the "muzzle of ice," this concrete detail requires too much twisting to make it relate to the main idea of the Man not making causal relationships.

Keep: He had a "pang of regret that he had not devised a nose-strap of the sort Bud wore in cold snaps."
Explanation: This concrete detail will be kept because it shows the Man realizing that he hadn't planned properly for the cold, but he is still not making the connection that there might be other consequences he failed to see.

Delete: He "was astonished at the swift numbness that smote them"—his fingers after they had been out for less

than a minute.
Explanation: This is a strong concrete detail. However, it provides the same information as the "sharp, explosive crackle that startled him." Both quotes express the idea of an unexpected cold, so having both would feel too repetitive. I personally preferred the wording of the "crackle" quote, so this one was deleted. I was left with three concrete details for my "Cold Temperatures" topic. This Example Throughout the Process paper will not be extremely long, with a total length of four pages double-spaced and only three body paragraphs, so two to three concrete details per topic is sufficient.

3. Write your commentary.

Now that you have your strongest concrete details, it is time to explain how your concrete details support your thesis, why they are important and what they mean. Commentary demonstrates your reasoning and always presents your own ideas in your own words. Usually commentary is placed after the concrete detail it is explaining. However, you can include commentary before the concrete detail for three main reasons: to switch up the rhythm of the paper, to introduce the readers to a particular view before they read the concrete detail itself, or to provide background information necessary to understand the quote and its relevance.

If you are unsure how to explain what you are trying to say, start off by writing "This concrete detail shows how…" or "This supports the thesis because…." Please note that while these phrases are helpful in planning and writing commentary, they are actually detrimental to include in your final draft. Using cliché phrases such as these in your final paper can be repetitive and make for uneven flow. However, once you have your rough draft, you can usually remove these introductory phrases and the rest of the commentary will stand successfully on its own.

When writing commentary, it is not enough to merely say "this supports my thesis" or "this is an example of my topic sentence." You have to explain why this particular fact is important to answering the prompt and how it supports your thesis. Readers don't want to draw their own conclusions. Instead, they want you to bring them through your thought process and lead them to *your* conclusions. See Box 5.2 for a demonstration of writing commentary in the Example Throughout the Process.

Box 5.2: Example Throughout the Process

Thesis: Jack London's "To Build a Fire" presents the protagonist's final downfall as his failure to assess the repercussions of his own decisions, including his lack of appreciation of elemental hazards, his failure to build fire and his insistence on traveling alone.

Topic 1: Elemental Hazards

Concrete Detail 1: "Fifty degrees below zero was to him just precisely fifty degrees below zero. That there should be anything more to it than that was a thought that never entered his head."

Commentary 1: The words "just precisely" imply that the temperature is only a temperature to the Man, nothing more and nothing less. He decides to venture out into this cold weather without thinking of any effects the temperature might have on his journey—in fact, a thought that "never entered his head." It is very telling that the

---

character, who is about to enter a wild and untamed land alone, does not even consider the temperature.

Concrete Detail 2: When he spat, "There was a sharp, explosive crackle that startled him" but he did not think any more of it.

Commentary 2: The words "sharp" and "explosive" are harsh, staccato words that imply violence, and the noise, due to the intense cold, surprises the Man. However, he fails to make any cognitive link between the violence implied by the sound that he did not expect and potential danger to himself.

Concrete Detail 3: He had a "pang of regret that he had not devised a nose-strap of the sort Bud wore in cold snaps."

Commentary 3: Early on, the Man recognizes that he is missing one piece of cold-weather equipment, but this still does not cause him to draw any further conclusions about the intense cold that he has never before experienced. Furthermore, regret is only described as a "pang," which suggests a small, unimportant feeling that will soon pass. Despite the fact that he has already realized he is not as prepared as he could be, he remains unwilling or unable to predict further repercussions to his decision to travel solo in such an extreme environment.

Explanation: The wording of these three concrete details is vital and the pieces of commentary discuss the connotations of specific words. For example, the sound of the words "sharp" and "explosive" is referenced, giving support for my argument that these words show the violence of the cold weather. Rather than merely referencing the plot, the commentary focuses on *how* London presents the story. Authors will use precise words and phrases with the intent of provoking a specific reaction from the audience. By looking at these literary tools, you can deconstruct the author's purpose and explain why a work is particularly effective. Because the Example Throughout the Process essay is persuasive, I wrote two to three pieces of commentary for each concrete detail. This gave me ample space to explain the importance of each concrete detail and show the connection to the thesis argument.

Topic 2: Failure to Build a Fire

Concrete Detail 1: He knows the importance of preventing the flame from being drowned in snow—this is why he lays down the larger sticks over which he makes his first fire.

Commentary 1: It is very clear that the man realizes how fragile a fire is, and how important this fire is to him. However, because he takes this initial extra effort to protect the fire, it is even more telling that he does not appreciate his precarious location under the snow-laden trees.

Commentary 2: Even more than building his fire under the snowy trees, the Man shows a reckless lack of foresight in pulling twigs for the fire off of the trees themselves.

Concrete Detail 2: Each time he pulled a twig off it was "an imperceptible agitation, so far as he was concerned," which aided the snow in falling and smothering his fire.

Commentary 2: The phrase "so far as he was concerned" tells the audience that, contrary to his previous statement that the shaking was "imperceptible," he could detect the shaking and chose to ignore the sign. The Man decided to pull twigs off of the tree without making the connection that the movement could cause the heavy snow to fall on his vulnerable fire.

Concrete Detail 3: Still, the man was "shocked" at the sudden snow fall.

Commentary 3: The word "shocked" reinforces the Man's lack of connection between his risky behavior and the devastating outcome. He did not think through his actions and therefore the result comes as a surprise.

Explanation: While commentary is usually placed after the concrete detail, in some cases it is useful to include a piece of commentary before the evidence. For the second concrete detail, I placed a piece of commentary before the quote to emphasize its significance. This practice also helps freshen up the rhythm of the paper. It is vital that the difference between concrete detail and commentary is clear, especially when you switch up the order, but when the concrete detail is a quote (as it is here) then this problem is eliminated.

You can also see that I've already started thinking about the order of the concrete details. In this topic, "Failure to Build a Fire," it is clear that the facts are in chronological order, starting with the Man building the fire, then feeding the fire, then his reaction to the fire dying. Having a logical order to your concrete details will help the overall flow of your essay.

Topic 3: Traveling Alone

Concrete Detail 1: "All a man had to do was keep his head...Any man who was a man could travel alone."

Commentary 1: The word "all" implies that keeping one's head is the only requirement to staying alive when traveling alone, suggesting that staying alive is a simple matter. A similar idea is expressed in the second phrase, where the phrase "any man" leads to the conclusion that this feat is not extraordinary. These statements go beyond confidence and boasting; they demonstrate the man's critical failure to accurately assess a situation. These statements seem more fitting to an afternoon jaunt, rather than someone about to travel the treacherous winter of the Yukon.

Concrete Detail 2: "The old-timer on Sulphur Creek was right, he thought in the moment of controlled despair that ensued: after fifty below, a man should travel with a partner" (after second fire).

Commentary 2: The phrasing of this sentence shows that even after failing to build his second fire, when faced with imminent death, the man continues to avoid facing the repercussions of his own failures by traveling alone. Although he realizes that a partner is vital in such a harsh environment, his thoughts still avoid any reference to him being in the wrong. The Man uses the phrase "the old-timer...was right," instead of using the converse by saying that he was wrong. In addition, he uses the detached third person when he states that "a man should travel with a partner." There is no acceptance of his own mistakes, no connection between his own fault and his current danger.

Explanation: Remember, this is still a very rough draft and the wording does not need to be perfect, as long as you include specific ideas. In this section, I included a note, "after second fire" in the second concrete detail, to give the context of the quote. In subsequent revisions, this phrase will be integrated into the main text of the sentence for a more formal presentation, but for this first very rough draft it merely serves as a reminder to include the context.

Takeaway Points

- Commentary simply explains, *in the writer's own words,* how a certain concrete detail supports the thesis.

- Informative essays require, on average, one piece of commentary for every two concrete details.

- Persuasive essays require, on average, two pieces of commentary for every concrete detail.

- Keeping and using only the strongest concrete details will make it easier to write commentary.

Chapter 6: Body Paragraphs

The body paragraphs include all the information that explains and supports your thesis—all paragraphs except the introduction and conclusion. Remember, your entire paper is linked together (see Box 6.1 Figure 6.1). Your thesis statement states your main argument (a direct answer to the prompt) and briefly introduces your supporting topics. Each supporting topic is expanded upon in one or more associated body paragraph(s).

The body paragraphs begin with a topic sentence (covered in Step 3 of this chapter), which clearly states the supporting topic and relates it back to the thesis. The concrete details provide inarguable evidence within the body paragraphs. Finally, your commentary will explain and connect that evidence directly to your thesis.

Now that you have your concrete details and your commentary, it is time to integrate them into cohesive paragraphs. Remember that this is still not the final draft, so grammar and flow do not have to be perfect.

1. Organize the body of the paper.
The order in which you present your supporting topics can be an effective tool in itself for upholding your thesis.

Box 6.1: Everything Supports the Thesis

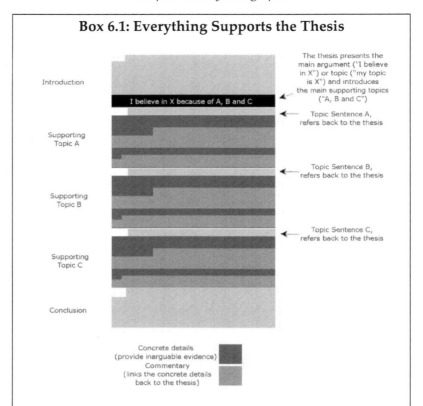

Box 6.1 Figure 6.1: Example Visual Diagram of an Essay

Explanation: This visual illustrates how every piece in an essay is directly related to the thesis. The thesis mentions each supporting topic and the topic sentence of each paragraph refers back to the thesis. Additionally, the commentary shows the relationship between the concrete details and the thesis.

A logical order of the body paragraphs can make the relationships between the supporting topics easier to understand. For example, if your topics each address a different time period, then a chronological order would make the most sense. If one topic presents "causes" and another addresses "effects," then "causes" should be placed before "effects." There may also just be a logical flow of ideas. Think about the progression of your topics. Is this the best arrangement they can be in?

Once you decide on the order in which you would like to present your topics, you will have to maintain consistency with that sequence throughout the paper. For example, if your order of topics in the body of your paper is "nature," "the Man," "the Dog," then your thesis and conclusion must also mention those topics in that order.

2. Add couplers to your concrete details.

Each body paragraph must have *at least* one concrete detail to provide strength to your arguments. Regardless of the type of concrete detail, it must be linked with the rest of the paragraph so it does not feel like it is free-floating. "Couplers" are the short linking phrases which can be placed before or after a concrete detail. A coupler located at the beginning of the sentence can also be called a "lead-in."

As you transform the concrete detail phrases or quotes you have collected into complete sentences, remember that your audience may not be familiar with your paper's subject. When you are first presenting potentially-confusing information, such as a new character you haven't yet introduced, the coupler should include background information to orient your reader (see Box 6.2). Different styles of concrete details require different styles of couplers, which is what this section will address.

Box 6.2: Example of Context for a Concrete Detail

Concrete Detail with Context Coupler: The Dog, the Man's only companion in his trek across the Yukon, had a "vague but menacing apprehension" from the outset (London).

Explanation: If this was the first time the character of the Dog was mentioned in the paper, a new reader who is not familiar with "To Build a Fire" might not understand why the Dog is important. A phrase such as "the Man's only companion in his trek across the Yukon" helps the audience understand the significance of this character. Even if a paraphrase was used instead of a quote, this coupler would be necessary to help orient the readers.

Integrated Quotations

Because an integrated quotation will be worked directly into a body paragraph, it is important that you have a seamless transition between your words and the quotation itself. A sentence with an integrated quote in it should always start and/or end with a coupler (a quote should never stand alone) and the sentence should be able to be read without the quotation marks and still sound natural (see Box 6.3).

An advanced technique for integrating quotations is to include your opinion in the coupler (see Box 6.4). This is an effective technique when working with quotations, because the concrete detail is clearly contained within the quotation marks and is distinct from your own words. This technique is much more difficult to use effectively in other forms of concrete details, such as paraphrases, where the line between coupler and concrete detail is not as clearly defined. Only use this technique if you can clearly differentiate concrete details and commentary.

Box 6.3: Examples of Couplers with Integrated Quotations

Integrated Quote with Coupler at Beginning: The Man thought to himself, "Any man who was a man could travel alone" (London).

Integrated Quote with Coupler at End: "Any man who was a man could travel alone," the Man thought to himself (London).

Explanation: Both types of couplers, before and after the quote, work equally well. The couplers here do not add any opinion and merely provide context for the quote. Usually your own words are separated from the quotation with a comma, as you can see in these examples.

Box 6.4: Example of a Factual Coupler vs. an Opinionated Coupler

Factual Coupler: The Man states that his accident "would delay him an hour" (London).

Opinionated Coupler: The Man *foolishly* states that his accident "would delay him an hour" (London).

Explanation: Both couplers, factual and opinionated, introduce the quote smoothly. Even when adding the opinion, the coupler still serves to provide context for the quote and is not too long. By adding the word "foolishly," the writer introduces the direction the argument will take. This is a great way to smoothly integrate your commentary and concrete details.

Block Quotations

Block quotations must always be introduced by a coupler phrase followed by a colon (":"). This coupler phrase signals to the audience the background and significance of the quote, so the readers are not disoriented. You may (and probably should) have commentary directly after this concrete detail, but you must *always* have a phrase of introduction before the block quote starts (see Box 6.5).

With block quotations as well, you have the option to include some opinion in the coupler phrase. Because your words are clearly separated from the concrete detail, there is no risk of confusion between which words show your personal opinion and which words are strictly concrete details.

Box 6.5: Example of a Block Quotation Coupler

Block Quotation with Coupler: The Man continues to deny his mistakes, despite mounting evidence:

> Those old-timers were rather womanish, some of them, he thought. All a man had to do was to keep his head, and he was all right. Any man who was a man could travel alone. But it was surprising, the rapidity with which his cheeks and nose were freezing. And he had not thought his fingers could go lifeless in so short a time. (London)

Explanation: This coupler provides a summary of the events surrounding this block quote. Even though this coupler does not include any obvious opinion words, it still directs the readers to one particular interpretation of the quote. This is useful because it signals to the readers what they should focus on in the quote itself.

Paraphrases, Summaries and Facts

If you have collected paraphrases, summaries or facts, they should currently be written in short phrases in your own words. Now they must be transformed into complete sentences. Just as with quotations, you should use couplers to introduce these concrete details and point towards their significance (see Box 6.6). If you use pronouns (such as "he," "she," "it," and "they"), make sure it is clear to whom you are referring.

Box 6.6: Example of Paraphrase

Example of a Paraphrase Concrete Detail: When the Man built his first fire, he built it on top of larger sticks he had laid down first.

Explanation: A paraphrase can make a compelling concrete detail if it is specific. This paraphrase also includes a coupler to provide context at the beginning of the sentence, reinforcing for the audience that we are talking about the *first* attempt to build a fire. Keep in mind that this coupler is *only* factual and does *not* contain any opinion. When paraphrasing, avoid opinionated couplers because the distinction between your opinion and the concrete detail is not clear.

Also remember that some of the concrete details you have gathered, especially the summaries, may be used as something other than a concrete detail in a body paragraph. For example, summaries are frequently used in the introduction of a paper or in the couplers for other concrete details to help give the audience context (see Box 6.7). As you are transforming these paraphrases, summaries and facts from a list of phrases into complete sentences, consider if there are any you want to use as couplers, in the introduction or in the conclusion.

Box 6.7: Examples of Using Summaries

Example of a Summary in an Introduction: The short story "To Build a Fire" by Jack London tells the tale of a man who decides to travel by himself through the Yukon in frigid temperatures. With only his dog for company, he ignores the advice of the Yukon veterans in town: to never travel alone. He ends up falling through ice and getting his legs wet, a fatal blunder in the sub-zero temperatures. Without a companion to help him, he has difficulties building a fire after his hands are frozen. The story ends with the Man freezing to death.

Example of a Summary Introducing a Quote: Even after breaking through ice and getting his legs wet to the knees, the Man remained resolute; "Any man who was a man could travel alone" (London).

Explanation: When a summary is used in the introduction, it can be several sentences and usually provides a summary of the entire topic or work. This is in contrast with a summary used to introduce a quote, which must be limited to a phrase or two in length. A summary is difficult to use as a concrete detail itself because it is often too vague or broad.

Interviews

There are two primary ways an interview can be used in an essay: in an objective style or in a descriptive one. The most common method is to include only short, relevant quotes as concrete details; this is known as an objective interview style (see Box 6.8). This method does not provide any additional details, such as the speaker's tone of voice, mannerisms or actions. This style can be useful because there will be little bias in the presentation of these quotes, resulting in a more detached, objective writing style.

Box 6.8: Example of an Objective Interview

Example of an Objective Interview Concrete Detail: Lydia, a native of the Yukon, recollected, "when I was young, it would get so cold outside that I was kept home from school—we didn't have enough money to buy me a proper winter coat."

Explanation: Just as you must quote any material taken from an outside source, so must you place quotation marks around anything your interviewee says. These words are concrete details. In this example, a coupler is used to introduce the interviewee who said the quote.

The second method to integrate an interview into an essay is called the descriptive interview method. This method is similar to constructing a story, where you incorporate additional details from the interview (see Box 6.9). Using a descriptive interview style makes a paper more relatable, helping the audience to imagine the scene as if they were present. However, there is always an inherent bias in what details you choose to describe. As a result, this style is often considered less objective and not appropriate for scientific or strictly informative papers.

3. Create topic sentences.

In this section, you will write the topic sentence for *each* body paragraph. The purpose of a topic sentence is to introduce the subject of your body paragraph and then

---

Box 6.9: Example of a Descriptive Interview

Example of a Descriptive Interview Concrete Detail: Lydia kept her eyes on her lap, twisting her tissue round her fingers, muttering "when I was young, it would get so cold outside that I was kept home from school—we didn't have enough money to buy me a proper winter coat."

Explanation: This second method is more like a story and it helps the readers to imagine Lydia; we can see how unhappy she is about this memory. This description grabs a reader's attention by giving the interview a vivid reality, but also makes the paper less objective.

---

explain how that subject is related to your thesis (and in turn answer the question posed by the prompt). A topic sentence should be only one sentence and readers should be able to read it, by itself, and gain a clear idea of what the following paragraph will be about. See the process of turning topics into topic sentences for the Example Throughout the Process in Box 6.10.

Box 6.10: Example Throughout the Process

Thesis: Jack London's "To Build a Fire" presents the protagonist's final downfall as his failure to assess the repercussions of his own decisions, including his lack of appreciation of elemental hazards, his failure to build fire and his insistence on traveling alone.

Brainstormed Topic 1: The Man does not make the link between the intense cold and the danger to himself.

Revised Topic Sentence 1: Even though the Man knows it is dangerously cold, he still does not make the connection that the elements could be fatally dangerous.

Explanation: The topic sentence is, at its core, a refinement of the topic brainstormed in Chapter 2. At this point, you are merely checking that it includes the topic of the paragraph and the relationship with the thesis, and that the wording is concise and specific. This topic sentence was revised to include both the main subject of the body paragraph (elemental hazards) and the relationship to my thesis (the Man doesn't think ahead and doesn't make causal relationships).

Sometimes you may have more than one paragraph per topic, but it is still vital that each paragraph has its own topic sentence. This sentence answers the questions: "What is the unique topic of this paragraph?" and "Why is this paragraph important?" The other topic sentences in this sample essay can be found in the final draft of the Example Throughout the Process (Appendix II).

4. Add transitions between paragraphs.

Your body paragraphs are almost done! Now we just need to add the "glue" between the topics. The purpose of a transition is to show the relation between adjacent paragraphs. These transitions can take the form of sentences, words or phrases, and can be at the beginning or end of a paragraph (see Box 6.11).

A transition at the beginning of a body paragraph will relate that paragraph to the previous one and will usually be a single word or a short phrase in the topic sentence. Transitions at the end of body paragraphs are used to flow into the following paragraph; these are often one full sentence.

At this point, the first draft of the essay's body is complete (see the body for the Example Throughout the

Process essay in Box 6.12). There are only two remaining paragraphs to write: the introduction and the conclusion.

Box 6.11: Example of a Transition

Example Transition between Two Paragraphs:
Paragraph 1 subject: Cold temperatures
Transition between the two paragraphs: Despite the cold, the man was undeterred from venturing out alone.
Paragraph 2 subject: The Man's insistence to travel alone

Explanation: The two paragraphs have distinct topics, but a relationship between them must be shown for a clear flow through the essay. This sentence creates a link between the two ideas and could be placed either at the end of the paragraph on cold temperatures or at the beginning of the paragraph on traveling alone. For examples of transition words, please refer to Appendix V.

Box 6.12: Example Throughout the Process

Thesis: Jack London's "To Build a Fire" presents the protagonist's final downfall as his failure to assess the repercussions of his own decisions, including his lack of appreciation of elemental hazards, his failure to build fire and his insistence on traveling alone.

Essay Body: Even though the Man knows it is dangerously cold, he still does not make the connection that the elements could be fatally dangerous. When introducing the protagonist, the narrator states that "Fifty degrees below zero was to him just precisely fifty degrees below zero...That there should be anything more to it than that was a thought that never entered his head." The words "just precisely" imply that the temperature was only a temperature to the Man, nothing more and nothing less. He decides to venture out into this cold weather without thinking of any effects the temperature might have on his journey—in fact, this thought "never entered his head." It is very telling that the character, who is about to enter a wild and untamed land alone, fails to consider the temperature as posing a hazard. At the beginning of the Man's journey he spat in the cold air, and there was "a sharp, explosive crackle that startled him," but he did not think any more of it. The words "sharp" and "explosive" are harsh and staccato words that imply danger; the noise, created from to the intense cold, surprises the Man. However, he again fails to make any cognitive link between the danger implied in the sound of his spit freezing instantaneously and the danger of the cold. After the Man starts traveling, his cheeks and nose begin to frost and he has a "pang of regret that he had not devised a nose-strap of the sort Bud wore in cold snaps." Immediately in his trip, the man has a direct consequence from the frigid temperatures but still does not draw any further conclusions about the intense cold that he has never before experienced. Furthermore, the Man's regret is only described as a "pang," which suggests a small, unimportant feeling that will soon pass. Despite already experiencing unexpected consequences, he still does not see any further repercussions to his decision to travel a long distance in such extreme conditions. After the Man falls through ice, he is forced to stop traveling and immediately make a fire to dry out his wet feet.

The Man knows the delicate nature of a new fire in the snow, yet he still does not take necessary precautions when building his first. During his first attempt to build a fire, he remembers the importance of preventing the flame from being drowned in snow—this is why he creates a bottom layer of larger sticks. This takes extra effort, especially in the chilling temperatures that are stiffening his fingers, and clearly displays the man's awareness of how fragile a kindling fire is and how reliant he is on its success. Even though he takes initial extra efforts to protect the fire, in the end he still fails to realize the dangers of building a fire under snow-laden branches. Each twig he pulled off caused "an imperceptible agitation, so far as he was concerned," which led to the snow falling. Even more of a mistake than building his fire under the trees, the Man yanks twigs from the snow-laden trees themselves. The phrase "so far as he was concerned" tells the audience that, in reality the shaking was not "imperceptible." Still, the man is "shocked" at the sudden snow fall that dashes out his best chance for survival. The word "shocked" reinforces the Man's inability to connect his irresponsible behavior to the dire outcome. Near his end, the man, shocked and dismayed, reflects on the benefits of traveling with a companion.

Even though the Man was warned against traveling alone, he does not appreciate the danger of his situation until it was too late. In response to the cautions of the old men in the town, he said to himself "All a man had to do was keep his head...Any man who was a man could travel alone." The word "all" implies that keeping one's head is the only requirement to staying alive when traveling alone, similar to the word "any" in the second phrase, leading to the conclusion that this feat is not even extraordinary. These are more than merely boastful statements, but instead demonstrate a critical failure to assess a situation. These statements seem more fitting to an afternoon jaunt and seem very out-of-place for someone about to travel the treacherous Yukon terrain in harsh winter weather, where the slightest misstep could mean tragedy. After the Man failed in his second attempt to build a fire, in despair he concludes that "The old-timer on Sulphur

Creek was right...after fifty below, a man should travel with a partner." Even when he realizes that a partner is vital in such a harsh environment, his thoughts still avoid any reference to him being in the wrong. He uses the phrase "the old-timer...was right," instead of the converse: admitting that he was wrong. In addition, he uses the detached third person when he states that "a man should travel with a partner." There is still no acceptance of his own mistakes, still no connection between his own fault and his current danger.

Explanation: The first draft of commentary (see the Example Throughout the Process for Chapter 5, Section 3) contained all the ideas present in this more polished version. To make this draft, however, the word choice was cleaned up and transition words and phrases were added. This helps create a smooth flow between the different concrete details and from one paragraph to the next. For example, at the beginning of the first body paragraph, I added the phrase "When introducing the protagonist, the narrator states..." Not only is this a nice coupler for the concrete detail, leading in to the quote, but it also gives the audience vital context: what part of the story and what character we are talking about. It also establishes the idea of the "narrator," highlighting that this paper will look at the way information is presented (by the narrator) in addition to considering the plot details.

When assembling everything together into paragraph form, many of the phrases had to be adjusted to prevent an awkward flow. For example, in the last paragraph (about traveling alone), one of the sentences was revised to improve flow.

The original commentary sentence was: "These statements seem more fitting to an afternoon jaunt, rather than someone about to travel the treacherous winter of the Yukon."

The revised commentary sentence is: "These statements seem more fitting to an afternoon jaunt and seem very out-of-place for someone about to travel the treacherous Yukon terrain in harsh winter weather, where the slightest misstep could mean tragedy."

The main idea is still the same, but the unique message of the concrete detail was emphasized to prevent the pieces of commentary in this paragraph from sounding too repetitive.

This draft isn't perfect. For example, the body paragraphs switch back and forth between the present tense and the past tense, which doesn't sound very smooth. However, this rough draft *shouldn't* be perfect. It's more important to focus on the organization and message at this point, rather than the grammar.

Takeaway Points

- List your supporting topics in the same order throughout the essay — the order of topics in the thesis should be the same as their order in the body paragraphs.

- Couplers are phrases that integrate your concrete details into your paragraphs and improve the flow of your writing.

- Each body paragraph must have a topic sentence, which includes the topic of the paragraph and how it relates to the thesis.

- Transitions are like "glue," connecting different ideas (such as unique body paragraphs) together for smoother flow.

Chapter 7: The Introduction

After the body of the paper has been drafted, it is time to create the introduction. The introduction has four main purposes: to spark the interest of the reader (this piece is called the "hook"), to provide important background information necessary to understand the rest of the paper, to present the main supporting topics and to showcase the thesis itself. The thesis should be the last sentence of the introduction.

In general, the length of the introduction should mirror the length of the paper. This is especially true given the need to overview the different topics discussed in the paper; papers that cover more material will require longer introductions. The supporting topics are often mentioned in the thesis, but if not, or if the topics need further explanation, make sure this information is included earlier in the introduction. This helps the readers gain an overview of the different sections of your essay and understand how they relate to your thesis. In general, think of your introduction as an inverted pyramid which travels from broad, general ideas, funneling into more specific ideas and finally into your thesis, which is the most specific statement (see Box 7.1 Figure 7.1).

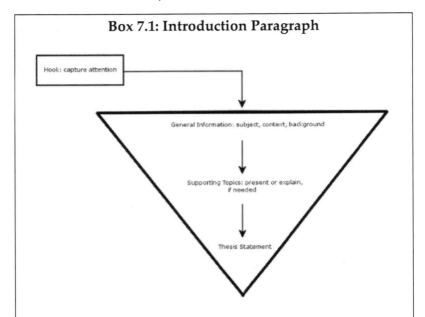

Box 7.1: Introduction Paragraph

Hook: capture attention

General Information: subject, context, background

Supporting Topics: present or explain, if needed

Thesis Statement

Box 7.1 Figure 7.1: Basic Form of an Introduction Paragraph

Explanation: After the hook has caught the readers' attention, the rest of the introduction funnels from the broadest points to the most specific: the thesis.

1. Provide context.

Providing context for your readers is vital in the introduction; this is where you introduce background information and set the scene. Your readers should have a clear idea of the setting, theories or characters involved in your paper. Imagine a friend reading your paper, a friend who has never taken this class or studied this topic. What questions would he/she have about your paper? What is necessary to understand the main idea of your thesis?

First, introduce the subject of the paper. If you are writing a literary analysis paper, include the name of the work and author, as well as when the piece was produced. If you are writing an informative paper, explain the paper's main subject and its context—what time period and geographical location does it exist in? If you are writing a technical paper, use this space to introduce any key theories and specific jargon that are vital to understand the main points of your paper.

Try to include only what is necessary to understand your paper, because too much unnecessary information can be overwhelming. After writing this section, re-read it and remove any details that aren't needed to understand your essay. See Box 7.2 for the introductory context used in the Example Throughout the Process paper.

2. Add the hook.

A hook can be the most exciting part of your paper—its purpose is to grab (or "hook") the attention of your audience. It can be a few sentences or even just a word or two, as long as it stands out and sparks the reader's interest. Even beyond writing a term paper, developing the skills to write a strong hook are crucial in writing scholarship applications, job applications, proposals, magazine articles, and more.

Think about a particularly memorable fiction book that you have read. Chances are that it started with a paragraph meant to entice you and make you want to read more. Did it jump into the middle of the action, segueing to flashbacks? Did it start with a provocative statement, a mystery, or a vivid description? If it was an introduction that made you want to keep reading then it was a successful hook.

> ## Box 7.2: Example Throughout the Process
>
> **Context:** In 1897, the American author Jack London joined the Yukon Gold Rush, looking for gold in the wilderness of Canada. His famous short story "To Build a Fire" tells the tale of a nameless man who decides to travel by himself in the dangerously frigid temperatures of the Yukon. With only his dog for company, he ignores the advice of more experienced men in town to "never travel alone" and ends up falling through ice and getting his legs wet. Without a companion to help him, he fails to make a fire to dry himself and as a result freezes to death.
>
> **Explanation:** I started this paragraph by introducing the author's name, time period and geographical location. I also noted the relevant point that Jack London participated in the Yukon Gold Rush, just as the main character in the short story does. I continued by introducing the name and basic plot of "To Build a Fire." All of this information is included in only a few sentences—it is vital that this section does not become too long.

For example, "To Build a Fire" starts when the Man has already left the town and is hiking through the desolate and foreboding landscape. The reader is enticed—why is he hiking in freezing temperatures? Why is he alone? This introduction appeals to the reader's sense of adventure as the main character tempts fate and battles against Nature. This encourages you to continue reading, answer these questions and discover what happens next.

When writing a paper, however, you do not have the luxury of a chapter-long hook—or even a paragraph-long hook! Your hook must be a few sentences at most, and ideally should be only one sentence. There are many different ways to hook your audience and some common choices include: quotes, unusual facts, short narratives, descriptions, rhetorical questions and sometimes even definitions. Remember, your hook should be directly related to your topic. Here are some common types of hooks:

Quotations

A quotation can be a strong way to start your paper. You can choose to either select a quote from outside material (make sure it is related to your thesis) or employ a particularly telling quote from your source material (see Box 7.3). Never use a quote that you will later use in the body of the essay.

Box 7.3: Examples of Quotation Hooks

Example Quotation Hook 1: "Winter either bites with its teeth or lashes with its tail." -Proverb

Explanation: This is an example of a related quote from an outside source. It would be effective because it connects the work to a larger picture, implying a greater significance to the message of the paper.

Example Quotation Hook 2: "He was quick and alert in the things of life, but only in the things, and not in the significances."

Explanation: This is a quote from the source document. This would make a good hook because it draws a very distinct image in the reader's mind, alluding to both the action and impending violence. This is a strong point to start with, one that a reader would be excited to pursue.

Avoid cliché, well-known quotes such as "I have a dream," "two roads diverged in the wood," and "all is fair in love and war." The purpose is to pique interest, so make sure you choose a quote that will stand out and not one that the reader has heard many times before.

Unusual or Interesting Facts

Surprising facts intrigue readers, but you must ensure that the fact relates to your topic and is somewhat obscure (see Box 7.4). A mundane fact will not serve the purpose of grabbing the readers' attention.

Box 7.4: Example of an Unusual Fact Hook

Example Unusual Fact Hook: The word "Yukon" means "the great river" in the language of the native Athapaskans.

Explanation: This fact is not only uncommon, but becomes morbidly ironic when connected to the short story at hand—falling into a literal river leads the Man to his death in the metaphorical river of the "Yukon." Explaining this connection would spark the interest of the readers.

Attention-Grabbing Stories or Descriptions

Stories and descriptions, true or imagined, tend to evoke a strong emotional response and lend a personal touch to your paper (see Box 7.5). A believable story told from first person, such as "I walked over the snow," is much stronger than a hypothetical story such as "Imagine you were walking over the snow," even if the story never actually happened to you. Try to limit your story or description to four sentences at the most and paint as vivid of a picture as possible.

Box 7.5: Example of a Story Hook

Example Story Hook: The snow crunched under my feet, flakes hitting my face and leaving behind small droplets. I hoisted my bag up, strap cutting into my shoulder. The taste of new snow was in the air and I eagerly turned my face upwards towards the looming mountains, ready to pit myself against the uncaring power of the Wilderness.

Explanation: The descriptive details, such as the "taste of new snow" and the "small droplets" of snow on my face, create a scene for the readers. This helps create the right mindset to appreciate the rest of the essay; it is easier to imagine the deathly cold of "To Build a Fire" if this idea has already been introduced so early in the essay. This hook also brings a personal touch to readers and plays off of their emotions and memories.

Rhetorical Questions

A rhetorical question is a question posed to the reader that you do not want a literal answer to. If the rhetorical question is unusual, it can make the reader stop and think of what his/her answer would be—this interaction between the reader and your paper can make this a very effective hook (see Box 7.6)

It is an unfortunate fact that rhetorical questions are often over-used and generally predictable, which is not what you want from a hook. To avoid the trap of a boring rhetorical question, try to get at the gut of the matter and make the question directly related to your thesis—the theme of your paper.

Box 7.6: Example of a Rhetorical Question Hook

Example Rhetorical Question Hook: Do you consider yourself a carefree impulsive spirit? Or a meticulous planner? While many people would gladly place themselves in the first category, in the savage environment of the Yukon such an outlook can have fatal consequences.

Explanation: This rhetorical question works well because it is specific—the reader is offered two defined choices. The reader is encouraged to consider what type of person he/she is, appealing to the reader's sense of self. Then, the rhetorical question and the reader's answer are directly connected to the topic at hand: the savage Yukon environment. If you use a rhetorical question, creating this connection to the topic is important—don't just drop the rhetorical question at the beginning of the paragraph by itself!

Definitions of Words

For the most part, avoid using a dictionary quote or a definition as a hook. There is rarely anything interesting or different about dictionary definitions (they are almost always what we expect the word to mean, even if you find a "secret" second meaning) and will not serve to spark the attention of the reader.

Definitions are better used as background information, in order to help the audience understand your topic or a particular point you are trying to make. You should only attempt to use a definition of a word as a hook when both the word and the definition are unusual and will pique the interest of the reader.

3. Introduce your supporting topics.

In many introductions, including an additional section about your supporting topics provides a critical overview of the paper to come. For some introductions, it may not be necessary; it can feel redundant or cause the introduction to be too long. If you included your supporting topics in the thesis itself, adding an additional section about the supporting topics will most likely not be necessary.

However, if your supporting topics are long or confusing, if their relation to your thesis is not immediately apparent, or if you decided not to include them in your thesis statement, it would be a good idea to present them in the introduction paragraph (see Box 7.7). You should not need more than one sentence to discuss each topic—remember that this piece is merely to familiarize the readers with your supporting topics. The sentences here will only provide a road-map of your paper for the readers. The body of the paper itself will go into depth and provide the concrete details.

Box 7.7: Example of Introducing Supporting Topics

Example Sentence Introducing Supporting Topics: The Man neglects to appreciate elemental hazards, fails to build fire and insists on traveling alone.

Explanation: This introduction to the supporting topics could be included just before the thesis and would work well if a revised, shortened thesis was used, such as:

Jack London's "To Build a Fire" presents the protagonist's final downfall as his failure to assess the repercussions of his own decisions.

Presenting the supporting topics separately and using

> a shorter thesis places a greater emphasis on the one main argument of the essay: the protagonist's downfall is his inability to understand repercussions of his decisions. However, this format also places a greater burden on you as a writer because you must keep a tighter hold on organization. Without the main supporting topics listed in the thesis, you must be very clear in defining the topics in the introduction and in the paper itself.

4. Assemble the introduction.

All of the pieces of your introduction—hook, background, presenting your supporting topics and thesis—should be complete and now it is time to combine them into a cohesive whole. Remember that the hook should be the beginning of the introduction, as it is the first impression the readers will have of your paper. After the hook, place the background information, funneling from the broadest points (the context, author, and/or theories), through the more specific points (themes, characters, topics and/or explanations of technical jargon). If you wrote a separate section presenting the supporting topics, this will be woven in here, towards the end of the background information.

Finally, the introduction paragraph will end with the most specific point: your thesis. Do **not** change your thesis to fit the introduction! If changes are needed to improve the flow, change the other parts of the introduction. As you assemble your introduction, keep the idea of an inverted pyramid in mind. You can see that, with the exception of the hook, the introduction starts with the broad background information, works towards more specific information and finishes with the thesis statement.

Take this time to make sure your introduction is not too long. Often, when you are building the background information and the hook separately, you don't realize how long the entire piece will end up being! Now that all the pieces are together, take the time to check the length and streamline anything that needs to be trimmed. The introduction for the Example Throughout the Process is included in Box 7.8.

Box 7.8: Example Throughout the Process

Assembled Introduction: Do you consider yourself a carefree impulsive spirit? Or a meticulous planner? While many people would gladly place themselves in the first category, in the savage environment of the Yukon such an outlook can have fatal consequences. In 1897, the American author Jack London joined the Yukon Gold Rush, looking for gold in the wilderness of Canada. His famous short story "To Build a Fire" tells the tale of a nameless man who decides to travel by himself in the dangerously frigid temperatures of the Yukon. With only his dog for company, he ignores the advice of more experienced men in town to "never travel alone" and ends up falling through ice and getting his legs wet. Without a companion to help him, he fails to make a fire to dry himself and as a result freezes to death. Jack London's "To Build a Fire" presents the protagonist's final downfall as his failure to assess the repercussions of his own decisions, such as neglecting to appreciate elemental hazards, his failure to build fire and his insistence on traveling alone.

Explanation: This introduction paragraph follows the typical inverted-pyramid formula. First, a specific rhetorical question is used to connect with the reader and

---

spark interest in the hook. Then, the broad ideas are laid out with background information on the author, narrowing down to the story itself. After the story has been introduced, the introduction becomes more specific by describing the plot points and finally presenting the thesis. This introduction has a word count of about 180 compared to the total essay word count of about 1500. This is a reasonable length; the introduction should always be shorter than a body paragraph, which holds true here.

Takeaway Points

- An introduction is comprised of four parts: the hook, the context, the overview of the topics in the paper and the thesis.

- The hook is the first sentence or two of the introduction and captures the readers' attention.

- Providing context for your topic is essential so the readers don't feel lost.

- The overview of supporting topics might be included in your thesis, or might be a short, separate section immediately before the thesis statement.

- The most important part of the introduction is the thesis, which is usually the last sentence of the introduction.

Chapter 8: The Conclusion

The last paragraph in your essay, the conclusion, is important because it serves to bring together all of your main points, leaving the reader with a memorable last impression. You should not introduce any new arguments or concrete details in the conclusion. If you thought of your introduction as an inverted pyramid, think of the conclusion as a pyramid right side up; together, they make an hourglass. In general, the conclusion should start at the most specific point: restating your thesis idea. Next, it funnels out to main points your paper presented, then it finishes by making a bigger-picture connection (see Box 8.1 Figure 8.1).

1. Summarize your main points.

An important part of the conclusion is the summary section, where you restate all of the important points in your essay without directly repeating any prior sentences. This summary section is particularly helpful in long papers, where readers may have forgotten some of your arguments; you now have the opportunity to remind them with a run-through of your supporting topics and thesis. Shorter papers, with fewer topics covered, often only need to rephrase the thesis and include a brief reminder of supporting topics (see Box 8.2 for the Example Throughout the Process).

2. Say why your readers should care.

Towards the end of your conclusion, you should add a "why all this is important" piece. At this point, apply your opinion or topic to the big picture, such as your life, the reader's life or society in general. If you are writing a persuasive paper, this is where you can include a "call to

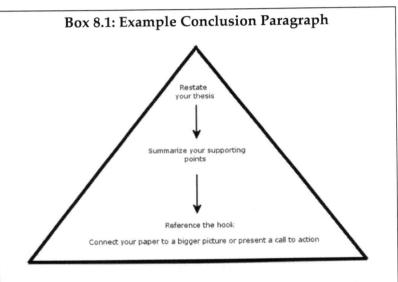

Box 8.1: Example Conclusion Paragraph

Restate
your thesis

Summarize your supporting
points

Reference the hook

Connect your paper to a bigger picture or present a call to action

Box 8.1 Figure 8.1: Basic Form of a Conclusion Paragraph

Explanation: The exact opposite of the introduction paragraph, the conclusion paragraph starts at the most specific point (the thesis) and funnels out to the more general points. The conclusion ends by taking this trajectory one step further and connecting your topic to a bigger picture.

Box 8.2: Example Throughout the Process

Summary of Main Points: The protagonist in this story does not make causal connections, as he fails time and time again to associate a known risk with any potential ramifications to himself. Even though the Man has proof of the extremely cold temperatures before he leaves, such as saliva freezing in the air with a "crackle," he still does not successfully assess the danger the extremely cold temperatures present. Furthermore, then he attempts to create fire, even though he knows how fragile and important the fire is, he still engages in several risky behaviors without thinking his actions through. Finally, his insistence on traveling alone leaves him no hope of rescue and even at the end he continues to deny his responsibility in choosing not to travel with a companion and the eventual fatal outcome.

Explanation: This conclusion summary starts with a restatement of the thesis, which is the most specific, important point of the essay. Then, the main supporting topics—cold, fire and traveling alone—are listed and again linked back to the thesis, driving that point home. One word is quoted to explain a supporting topic, but this is not new information because the quote itself was used as a concrete detail within the body paragraphs of the essay. Keep in mind that the order of topics is the same here in the conclusion as it was in the body of the essay, and as it was in the thesis itself. Staying consistent with this order maintains an organized, logical flow for your essay.

action." A "call to action" is a common device that challenges your readers to change or act in some way. Even if you do not include a "call to action," this is a vital opportunity to reinforce why the readers should care about your topic and opinion (see Box 8.3 for the Example Throughout the Process).

Box 8.3: Example Throughout the Process

Connection to the Reader: Jack London demonstrates the crucial importance of thinking through decisions and appreciating their consequences. All decisions have ramifications, however, not merely decisions in a snowy wilderness.

Explanation: In this example, Jack London's overall message is applied to the broader scheme of decisions and consequences in general. After reading this paper, many readers may mentally place this story in an "extreme survival only" box, but this last sentence widens the scope to all decisions and directly connects it to the reader.

---

3. Reference the hook.

In these last few sentences, you should also find a way to reference your hook. This brings a nice symmetry to a paper and reminds the reader of your very interesting introduction (the reason why many of your readers chose to continue reading), leaving them feeling satisfied. This reference should be just a phrase or a short sentence, much shorter than the original hook.

If you started off with a quote, give a short companion quote, reference a memorable phrase or word from the quote and link it to your opinion, or state something about the person who gave the quote.

If you started with an interesting fact or description, remind the readers of that and explain how it relates to the bigger picture, to your opinion, or to the readers personally. You can also end with a rhetorical question, as long as you keep it specific, interesting and relevant. See the Example Throughout the Process hook reference in Box 8.4.

Box 8.4: Example Throughout the Process

Hook Reference: No matter if you are an easy-going spirit or a careful planner, all decisions have ramifications, not merely decisions in a snowy wilderness.

Explanation: I added only a short phrase to reference back to the hook: "No matter if you are an easy-going spirit or a careful planner..." The initial hook was very short and a long reference back to it would be counterproductive. Instead, this phrase serves both to bring the essay full-circle as well as to reinforce that this essay is applicable to the reader on a personal scale.

---

4. Assemble the conclusion.

As your conclusion comes together, remember to maintain the "pyramid shape," with points specific to your essay placed at the beginning of the conclusion and bigger-picture statements coming at the end. Having a smooth flow through the conclusion is important, and usually this can be achieved by starting with the narrowest focus, working your way to broader statements, and ending with a call to action.

The most important purpose of the conclusion is to provide a sense of completion to your essay. Read it over: do you feel like the ideas in the essay have come to a natural close? Are any questions left unanswered? The complete Example Throughout the Process conclusion is assembled in Box 8.5.

Your paper's first draft is now complete! From here on out, you only have to smooth the rough edges and shuffle small details.

Box 8.5: Example Throughout the Process

Assembled Conclusion: The protagonist in this story does not make causal connections, as he fails time and time again to associate a known risk with any potential ramifications to himself. Even though the Man has proof of the extremely cold temperatures before he leaves, such as saliva freezing in the air with a "crackle," he still does not successfully assess the danger the extremely cold temperatures present. Furthermore, then he attempts to create fire, even though he knows how fragile and important the fire is, he still engages in several risky behaviors without thinking his actions through. Finally, his insistence on traveling alone leaves him no hope of rescue and even at the end he continues to deny his responsibility in choosing not to travel with a companion and the eventual fatal outcome. Jack London demonstrates the crucial importance of thinking decisions through to their consequences. No matter if you are an easy-going spirit or a careful planner, every decision has ramifications, not merely decisions in a snowy wilderness.

Explanation: This conclusion starts with the thesis statement and then gives a brief summary of the main supporting topics. None of the sentences in the conclusion are a direct restatement of any sentences earlier in the essay; instead, they reference the main ideas using new language to prevent the audience from feeling bored. The standard "pyramid" shape is used in this conclusion; this mirror of the "inverted pyramid" introduction gives a pleasant symmetry to the paper.

Takeaway Points

- A good way for a conclusion to start is by summarizing the thesis and main points in a few sentences.

- Towards the end of the conclusion, a short reference back to the hook lends a nice symmetry to a paper.

- A strong end to a conclusion will give a link to a bigger picture, provide a personal connection or include a call to action.

Peer review your paper

This is a good point to stop and look over your essay as a whole. So far, you've focused on creating each piece of your paper individually. Now, take some time to read it through, beginning to end, to check for the overall flow. Is your paper saying what you want it to? After you've looked over your paper and made any necessary changes, find someone to peer review it.

It's important to have an outside perspective look it over and ensure that it makes sense. At this point in time, the peer-reviewer should not focus on grammar. Instead, have your reviewer evaluate the ideas, content and organization/flow of your paper. After all, if you correct the grammar now but end up also reworking an entire section then you will have to recheck the grammar again. Any substantial changes to the content or organization should be finished before you continue to the editing process in the next few chapters, where we will focus on citations, grammar and formatting.

Chapter 9: Citations

In an academic paper, you must indicate where outside information, such as statistics or quotes, came from. This is called a citation. If you do not include a citation for information that is not original to you, then it can be considered plagiarism.

There are many different citation styles, including Modern Language Association (MLA), American Psychological Association (APA) and Chicago Manual of Style (Chicago). The different styles may require different information, may be presented in different ways and may even demand a different formatting style for your paper. Your professor will let you know which style of citation he/she prefers, but MLA style citations are the most common. This book uses MLA style for all examples, and this chapter provides an introduction to creating citations following MLA rules. Even though other citation styles vary slightly, for the most part they contain many of the same concepts and similar information.

There are two different places that sources must be cited in a paper: right after the information you included in your paper (in-text) and within a Works Cited section at the end of the paper. The in-text citation is short and serves two purposes: to inform the reader that what you've said is supported by an outside source, as well as to indicate which source in the Works Cited the information has come from.

1. Revise your in-text citations.

In Chapter 4, you included rough citation information for each concrete detail. Now it's time to polish that information into formal in-text citations (see Box 9.1). For most concrete details, including integrated quotations, paraphrases, facts and summaries, the in-text citation is placed at the end of the sentence(s). The final punctuation mark of the sentence (usually a period) is placed after the citation.

The standard MLA in-text citation includes the author's last name and the page number from which the fact was taken, placed within parentheses. Do not write "page," "pp," "p," or "pg" before the page number; only include the number of the page(s). By including the author's

---

Box 9.1: Example of Common MLA In-Text Citation

Common In-Text Citation: When Jack London was in his twenties, he "posed as an unlucky American sailor" who was stranded in London (Streissguth 57).

Explanation: The citation for this integrated quote is placed at the end of the sentence, just before the final punctuation (the period). The last name of the author ("Streissguth") and the page number ("57") were both available and included. If the concrete detail started on one page and continued to the next then the citation would reference both pages. For example, this citation would look like: (Streissguth 56-57).

---

name in the in-text citation, the readers can easily find the full citation in the Works Cited, and by including the page number, the readers can find the specific concrete detail in the original source.

In-text citations are the same for all types of concrete details with the exception of block quotations (see Box 9.2). Remember that with MLA style, a block quotation is any quote that is four lines or longer when inserted into your paper. The citation for block quotes is placed one space *after* the final punctuation mark, as opposed to integrated quotes where it is placed *before* the punctuation. However, the content of the in-text citation remains the same and contains the author's last name and the page number.

Box 9.2: Example of MLA Parenthetical Citation for Block Quotation

Block Quotation In-Text Citation: During the time Jack London spent in the depths of London, he realized the depths of poverty that existed, even there:

> In the East End, Jack saw the underside of life. The people of the East End had no work, no money, and no hope. Here, in the capital of one of the richest empires in the history of the world, people were going hungry and dying young...He watched as they picked through garbage looking for coins, clothes, or a crust of bread. (Streissguth 58)

Explanation: Remember that block quotations are not surrounded by quotation marks. Here, the block quotation ends with "crust of bread." Then, the in-text citation has been placed one space after the final punctuation park. No further punctuation is placed after the citation.

What if I have written the author's name in the sentence already?

Write only the page number within the parentheses if the author's name is stated in your own words in the text (see Box 9.3).

Box 9.3: Example of Citation with Author's Name In-Text

According to polar scientist Doctor Smith, the Yukon can be extremely cold in the winter (56).

What if there is no author name?

If the author is not given, something that is not uncommon in web sources, then write the title of the source within the in-text citation in the place of the author's last name (see Box 9.4). If the title is long, then shorten it to the first few key words so the audience can clearly understand to which of the sources in your Works Cited section you are referring.

Remember, underline or italicize the title if the source is a long work such as a novel, film, television series or magazine. However, if it is a short work such as an article or short story, then the title must be placed within quotation marks.

Box 9.4: Example of Citation with No Author's Name

The Yukon can be extremely cold in the winter (*Yukon* 56).

What if there are no page numbers?

It is possible that there are no page numbers for your source; this is common with electronic sources and films. If so, you will be citing the work as a whole and you do not have to include page numbers (see Box 9.5).

Box 9.5: Example of Citation with No Page Numbers

The Yukon can be extremely cold in the winter (Smith).

---

2. Create a Works Cited.

While in-text citations only contain a few pieces of information about the source, usually the author's name and a page number, your paper still must contain all of the information needed to find the exact source you used. This information is included in the full citation for each source. These citations are listed in a page called "Works Cited," which is a separate section at the end of your paper.

Writing citations can seem tricky because there are very strict guidelines for what information each citation must include. Furthermore, the information required for the citation changes based on the type of source (such as a book compared to a website). These guidelines can be helpful, however, because they give you an exact formula to follow when creating your citations.

There are four main types of sources that you may have to cite: journal articles, books, electronic sources and interviews. Use this guide to write full citations for every source with an in-text citation.

MLA Journal Article Citations

The basic format for a MLA journal citation is as follows, with an example in Box 9.6:

Last Name, First Name. "Article Title." *Journal Title* Volume Number.Issue Number (Publication Year): Beginning Page Number-Ending Page Number. *Database*. Medium Consulted. Date Accessed.

Box 9.6: Example of MLA Journal Citation

Smith, John. "Yukon Weather Patterns." *Environmental Journal* 78.2 (2006): 245-249. *Yukon Weather Studies.* Web. 23 June 2009.

Full Journal Citation Order

1. Author's Name: The names should be written last name first. The name should appear as it does in the source text.

2. Article Title: This is the name of the article itself and should be placed in quotation marks.

3. Periodical Name: This is the name of the journal and should be italicized.

4. Volume Number: Journals are released periodically throughout the year. Multiple journals are grouped together to form a "volume." Each volume is given a number.

5. Issue Number: Because multiple journals are grouped together to form a volume, each of those journals also receives its own number; this is the "issue" number.

6. Date of publication: This should be listed in the order of "Day Month Year," as specific as possible.

7. Page Numbers: In MLA style, write only the numbers, do not precede them with "p.," "pp.," or "pg." If no page numbers are given, write "n. pag." in the place of the page number.

8. Database Title: Include this if the article is a web source from a database. The database title should be placed in italics.

9. Medium of Publication Consulted: Write either "Print" or "Web."

10. Date Accessed: Only include this if you are citing a web source.

MLA Book Citations

The basic format for an MLA book citation is as follows, with an example in Box 9.7:

Last Name, First Name. *Book Title*. Edition. City of Publication: Publisher's Name, Year of Publication. Medium Consulted.

Box 9.7: Example of MLA Book Citation

Smith, John. "Yukon Weather." *Fatal Weather*. 2006 Edition. New York: Imaginary Publishing Company, 2006. Print.

Full Book Citation Order

1. Author's Name: The names should be written last name first. The name should appear as it does in the source text.
2. Title: This will be placed in italics.
3. Edition Used: If the edition is not given, omit this piece.
6. City of Publication
7. Name of Publisher
8. Year of Publication
9. Medium of Publication Consulted: This will be written either as "Print" or as the name of the e-book format, such as "Kindle file," "PDF file" or "EPUB file."

MLA Internet Sources Citations

The basic format for a MLA internet source citation is as follows, with an example in Box 9.8:

Last Name, First Name. *Article Title. Website Title.* Version or Edition. Publisher or Sponsor of website (use "*N.p.*" if this is unknown), Date of Publication(use "*n.d.*" if this is unknown). Medium Consulted. Date of Access.

Box 9.8: Example of MLA Internet Citation

Smith, John. *Yukon Weather. Weather Around the World.* 2008 Edition. International Weather Bureau, 2008. Web. 23 April 2009.

Full Internet Citation Order

1. Author's Name: The names should be written last name first. The name should appear as it does in the source text.
2. Work Title: Place the title in quotation marks if it is part of a larger piece or italicize it if it is an independent work.
3. Main Website Title: Include this only if it is different than the title of the work. If you include the main website title, italicize it.
4. Version or Edition: Include this only if relevant.
5. Website Sponsor: If this is not given, write "N.p." (standing for "not provided") in its place.
6. Date of publication: This should be listed as specific as you can find, but if it is not available then you should write "n.d." (to signify "no date").
7. Medium of Publication Consulted: Write "Web" for the medium of publication consulted.
8. Date Accessed: This will be written in the "Day Month Year" format.

MLA Personal Interview Citations

The basic format for a MLA citation for an interview you performed is as follows, with an example in Box 9.9:

Name of Interviewee. Kind of Interview. Interview date.

Box 9.9: Example of MLA Interview Citation

Jones, Margaret. Personal Interview. 26 April 2009.

Full Interview Citation Order

1. Name of Interviewee: This should be written last name first.
2. Kind of Interview: State the method of interview, such as "Personal Interview" (interviewed in person), "Written Interview" (interviewed via written correspondence) or "Telephone Interview" (interviewed over the phone).
3. Interview date: This will be written in the "Day Month Year" format.

Other Types of Citations

Included in this chapter are the citations for the most common types of sources. However, there are many other types of sources you may have to cite, such as encyclopedias, movies or blogs. For more specific information on writing citations, please refer to the most current *MLA Handbook*.

3. Organize your Works Cited alphabetically.

Organize your sources alphabetically by the first item in the citation. This is usually the author's last name but may be the title of the work, if no author's name is included. When alphabetizing, ignore any short starting words such as "a," "an" and "the."

4. Write an Annotated Bibliography, if required.

An Annotated Bibliography is much like a Works Cited section, but also includes one to two paragraphs per citation explaining some context, the significance of the source, why it will be useful for you, if there are any obvious biases, or any other important information about the source (see Box 9.10). Your professor will tell you if this is required.

Box 9.10: Example of MLA Annotated Bibliography

Example Annotated Bibliography Entry:
Smith, John. *Yukon Winters.* New York: Imaginary Publishing Company, 2005. Print.

This source is written by Environmental Scientist Doctor John Smith, and includes interviews with his colleague, renowned Polar Scientist Doctor Margaret Jones. The technical information in this source will be vital in explaining the weather patterns in the Yukon. However, both scientists are very liberal, so care must be taken that their political opinions do not come across too strongly in the factual information.

Explanation: This Annotated Bibliography is successful because it includes background of the author and the other significant contributor to the work. It then continues to illustrate the significance of the work and why it is important to the paper. The last sentence explains a possible drawback to using the source (both scientists have a strong liberal bias) and steps that should be taken so the

---

source is not compromised. For the Example Throughout the Process paper, which argues the reason behind the Man dying in the story, this liberal bias may not be as relevant an issue. However, if I was writing an informative paper about the dangers of the Yukon, then the bias may be critically important.

Takeaway Points

- A citation is a way to tell the readers where your concrete details come from.

- There are two types of citations that your paper must include:
  - In-text citations are short and included within the body of your essay, directly after concrete details.
  - Full citations are more detailed and listed at the end of your paper in the Works Cited.

- Different writing styles require unique citation styles.

Chapter 10: Grammar

At this point, the entire first draft of your paper should be completely written. However, correcting grammar is an easy way to improve the grade of a paper and should not be forgotten. This chapter provides some basic rules you can follow to improve the grammar in your papers.

There are a few exceptions to the rules in this chapter. If you are writing an informal narrative, personal reflection, dialogue or talking directly to the audience, then a conversational tone may be appropriate and some of the rules in this chapter may be ignored. For example, this book uses a casual tone and therefore does not follow every rule set forth in this chapter.

However, following these rules will help improve the vast majority of academic papers. This chapter is not a comprehensive source for all grammar rules; there are other sources that can provide detailed rules about grammar. Instead, this chapter will provide an overview of the most common mistakes and how to correct them.

1. Do not use contractions.

Contractions are shortened words such as "don't," "won't" or "can't." In formal writing, it is better to write out words in their entirety, such as: "do not," "will not," and "cannot." Contractions are considered very informal. Even though contractions are widely used in spoken English, even in a formal setting, they are not appropriate in formal academic writing.

2. Never use first or second person.

First person words include "I," "me," "my," "mine," "we," "us," "our" and "ours." Second person words include "you," "your" and "yours." Both first and second person words are considered too casual for a formal paper and should be avoided (see Box 10.1). Furthermore, using first person is often unnecessary; it is your paper, therefore the audience understands that the ideas contained within it are your own without using first person to state so directly. Very occasionally, you can use first and second person in the introduction or conclusion, but even then you must have a good reason.

Using second person can also be very imprecise. When a sentence starts "If you traveled to the Yukon during the Gold Rush," who do you mean by "you?" Do you mean men, women, gold prospectors, rich people, poor people, Native Americans, Russians, or another group of people entirely? Do you mean the reader specifically, and if so, can the statement be applied to all readers of your paper? It can be extremely jarring if a reader comes across "you" and the phrase is not applicable to himself or herself.

Finally, do not replace the first and second person pronouns in your paper with the pronoun "one". Using "one" as a pronoun usually sounds awkward and forced. Just rephrase the sentence, it's not too hard!

Box 10.1: Example of Rephrasing Second Person

Example with Second Person: When it is very cold out, *you should take* extra precautions.

Example without Second Person: When it is very cold out, extra precautions *are necessary*.

Explanation: In the sentence with second person, it is not clear if "you" refers to the reader, to everyone, or to a specific group of people. Rephrasing by adding the phrase "are necessary" eliminates this unclear "you," implies that this concerns everyone and makes this sentence feel more formal.

Example with First and Second Person: If it is extremely cold out, *I* would not suggest going outside by *yourself!*

Example with "One": If it is extremely cold out, *one* would not suggest going outside by *oneself!*

Example with Neither First Person, Second Person nor "One": If it is extremely cold out, *it* is not advisable to go outside *alone!*

Explanation: The first example, with both first and second person, feels very conversational and informal. Although it is grammatically correct, it does not feel appropriate for an academic paper. The readers know that all ideas in the paper belong to you, the writer, so referencing directly to yourself gives the impression that you are not certain; this is not very convincing.

The second example replaces "I" and "yourself" with "one" and "oneself," but this is both confusing and sounds stilted. The last example is the best because it maintains a formal tone, has a good flow and is the clearest.

---

3. Do not use colloquial language.

Colloquial language includes swearwords, local descriptive phrases (such as "raining cats and dogs" or "two peas in a pod") and slang words (such as "cool" when not talking about temperature). These words and phrases are discouraged not only because they are not formal, but also because their meaning can change based on interpretation (see Box 10.2). A word can have distinctly different meanings depending on the reader. If you describe a character in a book as "cool," do you mean that he was a daredevil? Athletic? Young, old, socially aware or socially impervious? For a higher quality paper, try to be as specific as possible in your language.

Box 10.2: Example of Removing Colloquial Language

Example with Colloquial Language: The Man thought that the men in the village were spinning yarns when they told him about the dangers of the Yukon.

Example without Colloquial Language: The Man thought that the men in the village were over-exaggerating when they told him about the dangers of the Yukon.

Explanation: The phrase "spinning yarns" can have several different meanings, including "telling lies," "relating fun stories" and "exaggerating the truth." The meaning is unclear and the phrase itself is informal, so replacing it with "over-exaggerating" is a much better choice.

---

4. Maintain consistent verb tenses.

A verb tense refers to how you are referring to the timing of events: did they happen in the past (past tense), are they happening now (present tense), or will they happen in the future (future tense)? Once you choose a verb tense for your essay, be consistent with this verb tense throughout the paper. If you are writing an informative paper about a historical subject, stay in the past tense for the entire paper. When describing events from a book, you should use the present tense, called the "literary present." This is because, theoretically, all the events in a book are happening continuously at the same time, so you should use present tense to describe them (see Box 10.3).

Box 10.3: Example of Correcting Mixed Tenses

Example with Mixed Tenses: The Man *strides* across the Yukon. He *looked* at the Dog's breath creating a cloud against the sky.

Example of Consistent Present Tense: The Man *strides* across the Yukon. He *looks* at the Dog's breath creating a cloud against the sky.

Explanation: In the first example, the order of events is not clear because the verb tenses change from the present to the past. To remedy this, both tenses are written in the present tense. This tense was used because the passage describes events from a book, which requires the present tense ("literary present"). Now, the order of the events in the sentences shows the order of events in the story: first, the Man walks, then the Man looks at the Dog's breath.

---

5. Be consistent with your pronouns.

In spoken English, pronouns ("I," "you," "he," "she," "it," "we," "they") can be flexible. For example, in spoken English you might say *"Someone* has hypothermia; *they* should be taken to the hospital." In written English that is not grammatically correct because "someone" is singular (refers to one person) while "they" is plural (refers to two or more people). This can be easily fixed either by *"Some people* have hypothermia; *they* should be taken to the hospital" or *"The boy* has hypothermia; *he* should be taken to the hospital." This change is important because it clarifies if you are talking about multiple people (the first possible solution) or one person (the second possible solution). In written English, it is important to make sure all of your pronouns agree (see Box 10.4).

Box 10.4: Example of Revising Pronoun Use

Example of Inconsistent Pronoun Use: The *men* in the village warned the Man against traveling alone. *He* said to always bring a companion when traveling in the cold.

Example of Consistent Pronoun Use: The *men* in the village warned the Man against traveling alone. *They* said to always bring a companion when traveling in the cold.

Explanation: The first example creates confusion. We are not sure if the "He" in the second sentence is referring to the Man, the old men giving the advice or one old man in particular. The second example makes this undeniably clear. By saying "they" all doubt is removed; it must be referring to the old men.

---

6. Write out whole numbers under 100.

When you are creating an academic paper, any whole number under 100 should be written out (see Box 10.5). This means that you should write out "three" instead of "3." However, "3.7" can stay in numeral form because it is not a whole number and would be too long and confusing to write out in words. There are a few exceptions to this rule, however. Always use the numeric form (write the numbers) for money, percentages, dates and addresses. Also, if you write a list of numbers and one or more of them must be written in numeric form (for example, if one of the numbers is a decimal), then the entire group or section should be written in number form to maintain consistency.

Box 10.5: Example of Writing Numbers in Text

Example with One Whole Number: Read the following *three* short stories before you write your final synthesis paper.

Example with a Group of Numbers: The team packed *14* apples, *5.5* bags of potatoes and *7* bags of flour.

Explanation: In the first example, "three" is the only number in the sentence. It is a whole number and does not fall under any of the exceptions (it is not referring to a decimal number, money, a percentage, a date or an address), so it is written out. In the second example, there are three numbers used within the sentence. While they are all under 100, one of the numbers is a decimal and must be written in numeric form. According to the last rule listed above, if one number in a group or section is written in number form then all of the numbers must be as well.

---

7. Choose precise words.

The earlier you start thinking about using specific word choice, the easier your revision process will become. Using detailed language helps prevent the audience from being confused, is more convincing and paints a more vivid picture of your topic (see Box 10.6). Never use the words "a lot," "good," "bad," "thing" or "stuff." Instead, use clear words to mean exactly what you are trying to say.

Box 10.6: Example of Improving Word Choice

Example with Weak Word Choice: The Man didn't bring a lot of stuff with him.

Example with Decent Word Choice: The Man brought little wilderness survival gear.

Example with Strong Word Choice: The Man barely even brought the bare necessities to survive in the wilderness.

Explanation: There are two areas that can be improved in the example with weak word choice. First, the phrase "didn't bring a lot" is fairly vague—is this a good thing or a bad thing? How much is "a lot?" Did the Man bring a medium amount or a small amount? In the decent example, this phrase is replaced with "brought little" and clarifies the quantity. In the strong example, this is replaced with "barely even brought," which clearly conveys the writer's opinion that this is a paltry amount and is very small.

   The second area to improve in the weak word choice example is the word "stuff." The word "stuff" is vague and is not clarified in this sentence. This is replaced in the decent example with "wilderness survival gear." This is a specific phrase and tells the audience directly what this sentence is talking about. In the strong example, the phrase "the bare necessities to survive in the wilderness" is used. This is even more specific and clearly signals that the items in question are not elaborate, unnecessary items but are the fundamental basics needed to enter the wilderness.

---

8. Describe using your senses.

Every paper, no matter the type, will include some descriptions. It is vital that these descriptions are vivid and memorable in order to paint a clear scene for the readers. Think of painting a picture; your essay is a black-and-white scene and the senses are the colorful paint. The more vibrantly you describe the scene, the better the picture will form in the readers' minds and the stronger association they will have with your writing. Effective descriptions can separate mediocre papers from memorable ones. Using more senses than just one when illustrating a scene or object can bring the subject to life for the reader and can make the portrayal stand out.

For example, when describing a scene, was there a smell in the air? Were there memorable sounds or any background noises? Did you taste anything? Taste can be more metaphorical as well, such as "the dog tasted winter in the air" or "the taste of defeat was bitter." Can you physically feel anything (cold, the carpet under your feet, were you holding anything)? Finally, sight—was there anything that caught your eye? By using more senses to describe a situation, your writing will be more memorable and create an inclusive experience for your readers (see Box 10.7).

Box 10.7: Example of Improving Descriptions

Example with a Simple Description: I walked on the snow, carrying a backpack and looking at the trees. This weekend would be my first time snow-camping and I thought about everything I needed. It looked like it was going to snow again and I turned to the mountains.

Example Description Appealing to the Senses: The snow crunched under my feet, flakes hitting my face and leaving behind small droplets. My heavy pack had begun to cut into my shoulder, so I hoisted it up further in a futile attempt to avoid the discomfort. I took a deep breath and inhaled the fragrant smell of pine. This would be my first weekend snow camping. I ran through everything I needed once again, checking the list mentally against the items in my pack. The taste of winter was in the air and I eagerly turned my face upwards, towards the oncoming mountains.

Explanation: In the second description, words with all five senses are used. For example, taste was evoked with the "taste of winter," feeling was brought in with the backpack strap "cutting into my shoulder," and hearing was described as "the snow crunched." A specific description will usually be longer, which will help create a more vivid picture in the audience's mind. This second description is more effective because it gives the readers a clear image. Through the given details, the readers can draw a scene based on similar memories of camping, being in the snow, being in the mountains, or other related experiences. This creates a relationship between the description and the readers, drawing the readers in and making them feel like the story was directed at them personally. You do not need to include all five senses in every description; this can feel repetitive and dull after a time. However, it is important to try to include at least two senses when illustrating an important scene, as it will make the passage stronger.

Takeaway Points

- Narrative papers do not have to follow all grammar rules; their purpose is to tell a story, so the rules are more flexible.

- Informative and persuasive essays should never use informal language, including contractions or slang.

- Informative and persuasive essays should avoid using first or second person (words such as "I," "you," "we").

- For all types of papers, including narratives, make sure your verb tenses are consistent.

- Be specific and vivid with your descriptions.

Peer review your paper again

After you have reviewed your own grammar, it is a good idea to have it looked over by a peer for another opinion. A fresh pair of eyes will be able to spot grammatical errors you may have missed. The peer editor will also be able to critique the overall flow and depth of your paper, not just grammar. You still have the power to substantially change your paper if you feel it is necessary at this point. However, remember that if you do, you will have to go back a few steps. Ideally, your revisions at this stage should focus on surface flaws such as flow, grammar and small points of clarification.

Chapter 11: Formatting

Formatting is the last step before your paper is completely done. While reviewing grammar involved changing the paper itself, formatting will not change the paper's content, but simply affect its presentation on the page.

1. Adjust font and text size.

The font is the style of the typeface used; it's basically what the letters look like. For MLA-style papers, the font should be clear, easy-to-read and professional looking, never looking like handwriting. The italics and bold words should be easily distinguished from the rest of the text. Times New Roman is the most common font, but others such as Arial are also appropriate.

The text size is the size of the letters. For all MLA-style papers, the text size should be 12. This includes the title, block quotations and the Works Cited. Beyond being the required font size according to MLA style rules, a text size of 12 is also a good balance between two sides. First, it is large enough for easy reading. Second, it is small enough to look professional and to be an efficient use of paper.

2. Verify margin and indentation sizes.

The margins refer to the white space around the border of your paper. Their size is dictated by the writing style, but usually one inch margins are accepted as the norm. This is the required margin size for both MLA and APA styles.

Every time you start a new paragraph, the first line of the paragraph must be indented, resulting in the text starting further to the right than the rest of the paragraph. This is different than in books or newspaper articles, where the first paragraph of a section may not be indented. In contrast, every new paragraph in an academic paper must be indented to the right by one-half inch (this is usually the default for the "tab" key). This helps distinguish paragraphs from each other. For MLA-style papers, do not include empty lines (do not press "enter" or "return" multiple times) between paragraphs. The paragraphs must follow one another directly, with each new paragraph indented; this is usually the style used in books, newspapers and magazines.

Remember that if you have block quotations, they need special formatting. Block quotations are flush with the regular right-side margin, but have an additional one inch of margin on the left side. This means that altogether, they have two inches of margin on the left side. The first line of the block quotation never has any additional indenting (do not press "tab" for the first line of the block quotation). However, if the block quotation has any further new paragraphs, the first line of each new paragraph will be indented an additional quarter-inch (see Box 11.1).

Box 11.1: Example Block Quotation Formatting

Block Quotation: Despite mounting problems, the Man experienced a renewed sense of hope:

> When he touched a twig, he had to look and see whether or not he had hold of it. The wires were pretty well down between him and his finger-ends.
>
> All of which counted for little. There was the fire, snapping and crackling and promising life with every dancing flame. (London)

Explanation: The first sentence, "Despite mounting problems...," serves to introduce the block quotation. Since it is not part of the block quotation itself, this sentence only has the standard one inch margins. Once the block quotation has begun, the left margin measures two inches while the right margin remains one inch wide. This block quotation spans two paragraphs. "All of which..." is the beginning of a new paragraph in the original text. In the block quotation, this line is indented an additional quarter-inch to signal the start of a new paragraph.

---

3. Double space the paper.

There are two main styles of spacing: single and double. With single spacing, there is no space between the lines of text. This format is often used in professional writing, such as in books, newspaper articles or scientific reports. However, in academic writing you should use double spacing unless specifically instructed otherwise. With double spacing, the lines of text are more spread out. This serves two purposes: it makes it easier for someone (such as a professor) to write a comment on the page and it improves readability of the paper. Many professors read numerous papers in a row and this helps make the paper easier to read. Regardless, double spacing is also required by most academic writing styles, including MLA style.

To change your format to be double spaced, do not press "enter" after every line. Instead, highlight the text and find the proper option to change, usually under the "Formatting" section of your Word Processor. This option will often be called "Line Spacing" and must be set to "double."

4. Include a proper heading.

The heading is the important identifying information at the top of the paper. For MLA-style papers, the heading should include, on separate lines: your full name, the name of your instructor, the title of the course and the date (see Box 11.2). The heading should be aligned flush with the left margin of your paper. The heading should be in the same font and size as the rest of your paper. It should not be bolded, italicized or underlined.

Box 11.2: Example Heading

Martha Smith
Professor R. A. Brown
Genealogy 101
January 21, 2001

---

5. Add a header or a footer.

Due to the one inch margins around your paper, there is blank space above and below the text of your paper. A "header" can be included in this blank space above your paper, while a "footer" can be in this blank space below your paper. The header or footer often contains your name, the page number of your paper or the title of your paper. Whether you should use a header or footer, and what information you should include, is dictated by the writing style you are using.

Many styles, including MLA style, require you to include your last name and the paper's page number in the header. This header should be in the right upper corner of each page. For example, if your last name is "Smith," in the upper right corner of the first page you would write "Smith 1," on the second page you would write "Smith 2," and so on.

To add a header, find the "Header and Footer" menu in your Word Processor. This menu may be under the "Insert" option. Select "Header" and type your last name followed by a space. Then click the "Page Number" button and follow the prompts to automatically add the page number to each page (steps may vary depending on your Word Processor). Now the correct information is in the header, so align it to the right side of the page (using "align text right" in the "Paragraph Formatting" section) and the header is finished.

6. Write a simple, correctly formatted title.

The purpose of a paper's title is to simply and clearly convey the topic of the text. The best academic titles are not artsy, joking or elusive references. You should not use first or second person words in the title.

The title should be in the same font and size as the rest of your paper and should not be bolded, italicized or underlined. It should be centered, and the first letter of every important word should be capitalized. Unimportant words, such as "a," "an," "the," "and," "but," and "or," should not be capitalized unless they are the first word of the title.

Do not include a separate title page unless specifically instructed to do so. As this is not part of standard MLA formatting, there is no set way to create one. However, if you are asked to create one with little guidance, start by creating a new page at the beginning of your paper. On this page, about one third of the way down, write the title of your paper. Two lines below that, write your name. One inch from the bottom of the page, write the professor's name, the course title and the date, each on its own line (this is the same information that is included in the heading). All of the text on the title page should be centered, should be written in size 12 and should use the same font as the rest of your paper (see Box 11.3 Figure 11.1).

7. Format your Works Cited section.

Many citation styles share similar rules for the Works Cited section. The following guidelines are true for MLA style papers and many other styles. However, different citation styles can have distinctly different ways of formatting the Works Cited section, even if only nuanced differences. If your paper is not written in MLA style, take these suggestions into consideration and consult a guide for the specific writing style you are using.

The Works Cited section will always start on a new page and will be the last section in your paper. Place the title, for MLA style papers this will be "Works Cited", centered at the top. This page should be double spaced — the same spacing as the rest of your paper — and should also have one inch margins. Format the citations on your Works

Box 11.3: Title Page

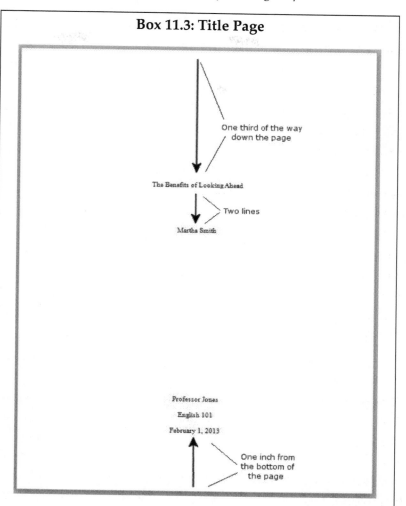

Box 11.3 Figure 11.1: Example Basic Title Page Formatting

Explanation: Here, the title ("The Benefits of Looking Ahead") is placed one third of the way down the paper. The author's name, "Martha Smith," is two lines below the title. At the bottom of the page, flush with the bottom one inch margin, is the rest of the heading information: the professor's name, course title and date.

Cited page with hanging indentation. Hanging indentation requires the first line of each citation to be flush with the left margin, but if the citation continues onto a second or third line then those lines are indented by one half of an inch (see Box 11.4). Even Annotated Bibliographies are formatted with hanging indentation, where the first line of the full citation is flush with the left margin and the rest, including the annotation, is indented.

Box 11.4: Works Cited

Example MLA Works Cited Page:
Works Cited

Jones, Margaret. "Northern Weather." *Fatal Weather, a Desk Reference*. 4th ed. 2008. Print.
Smith, John. *Yukon Weather. Weather Around the World*. 2008 Edition. International Weather Bureau, 2008. Web. 23 April 2009.

Explanation: This works cited begins with the title, "Works Cited," centered at the top. The entries are alphabetized by the first word of each citation: the authors' last names ("Jones," then "Smith"). The second citation is more than one line long, so the second line is indented by a half inch. This means that this line is one and a half inches away from the edge of the paper (the one inch of the margin plus a half inch additional indentation).

Takeaway Points

• Use text size 12 and an easy-to-read font such as Times New Roman.

• Use one inch margins around your paper.

• Use double spacing.

• The heading should be in the upper left corner of the first page of your paper and should include four items: your name, your professor's name, the course title and the date.

• The header should be in the upper right corner of every page and will include your last name and the page number.

• The title should be short, centered and in the same font and text size as the rest of your paper.

• The Works Cited should be formatted with hanging indentation, where the first line of the citation is flush with the left margin and all subsequent lines are indented by one half inch.

All of these points are true for standard MLA formatting. If you are using a different formatting style, consult and follow an appropriate guide.

Chapter 12: Narrative Essays

Thus far, this book has focused on general rules for writing informative and persuasive essays. The purpose of a narrative story is to tell a story, rather than persuade or inform an audience, and as a result this type of essay requires a different approach. While all essays should have a sense of focus, the point of a narrative essay is to entertain, not to prove or explain one particular point.

Informative and persuasive essays have fairly rigid organizational plans: beginning with an introduction, starting each body paragraph with a topic sentence, and so on. However, the writing method for narrative essays is much more flexible, giving you the power to forge the story in a way of your choosing. As such, the steps to guide you in creating your narrative essay are much broader than those for the informative and persuasive essays.

If you have not yet read Chapter 1: The Prompt, do so now and make sure that you have a firm understanding of what information to take away from the prompt. The Example Throughout the Process, for this chapter, will be a relatively short narrative responding to the prompt:

"To Build a Fire" depicts a conflict between Man and Nature. Using vivid sensory imagery, describe a time when you experienced a conflict with Nature. Was there a clear winner in the conflict?

1. Brainstorm and choose the focus of your narrative.

Brainstorm different possible events for your narrative to focus on, as suggested in Chapter 2, Step 2. After you have several options, eliminate any that do not directly respond to the prompt. When choosing the one to use for your paper, find the one with the strongest specific sensory memories. Select a memory with vivid details related to the events, such as a vivid color, background sounds, specific pieces of dialogue, memorable smells, a physical feeling, an emotional feeling, or even a particular taste. See the Example Throughout the Process for this practice in Box 12.1.

Box 12.1: Example Throughout the Process

Brainstorming with a List:
Times I have conflicted with Nature:
- When I became violently sea sick while fishing
- When I went snow camping
- When I hiked a very high mountain and ended up with a severe case of tendonitis

Explanation: I have the strongest memories of the time when I went snow camping and can clearly recall the sharpness of the cold air, the crunch of the frozen snow and the blue of the mountains. Clearer recollections will naturally lead to more vivid descriptions, so the second option of this list is my best choice for this prompt.

---

2. Write a thesis.

Even though you are not arguing a point or explaining an academic topic, it is still necessary to write a thesis statement. This ensures that all ideas in your narrative are related to a central theme and that the main focus is clear. Write one sentence that summarizes the most important part of the story you want to tell (see the Example Throughout the Process thesis in Box 12.2).

You may choose not to include this sentence in the final draft of your essay. A narrative usually does not need to include a formal thesis statement and often will flow better without one. However, writing a thesis at this point will be critical in defining your focus and ensuring that all pieces of the story revolve around this main point.

Box 12.2: Example Throughout the Process

Thesis: I was overconfident during my first time hiking with skis, which led to a conflict with the severe snow storms but ended with me feeling like a winner, due to my gained experiences, as I headed back to my car.

Explanation: This sentence not only summarizes the main point of the story, but also answers all of the questions contained in the prompt. The final draft of this narrative does not include this thesis statement, but it was important to create one because as I drafted the story I could check at every point to ensure everything was on-topic. If a point did not directly correspond to the thesis, that meant it was an unnecessary tangent and most likely did not belong in the story.

---

3. Create an outline.

Unlike an informative or persuasive essay, a narrative requires a plot, or a plan of how all the events in your story are related. What major events occurred? What should the focus of the story be? Even if you are relating several events, choose one to be the central event. Having all other events tie in or lead up to this main event will enhance a sense of cohesion in your story.

After creating your main plot points, take a moment to brainstorm strong sensory memories associated with each. Try to jot down a "snapshot" of sensory data relevant to the event; this will help you create detailed descriptions throughout your story. See the main plot points and sensory memories for the Example Throughout the Process narrative in Box 12.3.

4. Write the first draft.

Refer to your outline and draft what was happening as you go through the events in your mind. At this point, do not focus on having perfect word choice or the smoothest descriptions, but do try to be as specific as you can with situations and examples. Remember to incorporate the sensory memories you brainstormed and try to include descriptions from at least two senses for each important event in the story.

As you start your draft, consider if you need an introduction paragraph or if you should start in the thick of the story. In contrast with persuasive and informative essays, not all narrative essays need an introduction paragraph. Sometimes it serves your tale better to jump right into the action; however, if you are trying to illustrate a big-picture point then it may be beneficial to set up this connection in an introduction paragraph. Also remember that the audience should not need to already know any specific, technical information to understand your story. If you are including technical information, or

---

Box 12.3: Example Throughout the Process

Plot Points with Associated Sensory Memories:
1. Arrived at trail head, put skis and pack on. Very optimistic at this point.
   - The backpack was heavy and dug into my shoulders
   - It was difficult to balance on the skis
2. Lost the trail, it was snowing hard, decided to head over a ridge. Terrified of the unknown situation.
   - All sound was muffled by the snow
3. After struggling upwards for three hours, the avalanche danger became too high and we retreated down the hill. Relieved at this decision.
   - Small avalanches were starting all around us, with sheets of snow sliding down the incline and exploding against trees below
4. Camped for the night. In the morning, the avalanche danger was still high, so we hiked back out and went home. Satisfied with the experience.
   - The fragrant smell of soup for dinner
   - Felt much more balanced on skis

Explanation: In this outline, I included the most important plot points. These points are distinct because each represents a different point in the story and a unique emotion, demonstrating how the mood shifts throughout the story. I also included sensory memories for each plot point. The first draft includes much more detailed and varied descriptions, but in the outlining process these were the ones that jumped out of my memory.

---

if your story involves several characters, make sure that you provide any necessary background information. You may choose to include this information in an introduction paragraph or you may disperse it throughout your story, whichever would suit your narrative better.

Create your first draft now, focusing on relaying specific situations without worrying about the word choice. Refer to Box 12.4 for the first draft of the Example Throughout the Process essay.

Box 12.4: Example Throughout the Process

The fresh snow squeaked underfoot as my friend and I arrived at the trail-head, where we would start our hike up a snowy valley. This was to be a trip of many firsts: my first time snow camping, my first time hiking on skis, even my first time hiking in the snow. Out of my pack I grabbed my "skins," pieces of specialized material that would be fastened to the bottoms of my skis to prevent me from sliding backwards, making it possible for me to hike uphill in deep snow without sinking.

I took a few steps forward on the unwieldy skis, the heavy pack shifting my center of gravity. My friend took off and I trailed behind, skis slipping sideways every few steps. A heavy pine scent hovered in the air and a few pieces of snow touched upon my nose. The snow was laying down a thick blanket over the landscape, muffling every sound. Snow dusted my lashes and turning to small drops of water from the heat radiating off my skin. My pace slowed as I saw my friend stopped ahead, head craning upwards. He turned towards me as I neared.

"We've lost the trail with all of this snow. We'll have to go over the ridge here."

I nodded, unease curling in my abdomen as I considered the steep incline; I had barely managed to master moving on the nearly flat path. The first few switchbacks were not much more difficult than what we had just traversed, but as twilight began to fall and the snowfall grew heavy, the path became a near vertical climb. Refusing to admit defeat, our pace slowed to a crawl as we crept up the slope. I moved carefully, sliding back with every step despite the skins.

We froze as a buildup of loose snow began to move as one mass down the mountain and crashed against a thick tree trunk. My friend turned towards me and inclined his head back down the way we had come. I nodded—the avalanche danger was too high and we had to turn back after three hours of suffering up the ridge.

We took off our skis to avoid the dangers of skiing in dangerous conditions and then half-slid, half-struggled down the hill in waist-deep snow. Spotting a place to make camp among a circle of tall trees, we quickly set up the tent to get out of the blizzard. As the wind whipped the branches far above and the snow lashed against the side of the tent, we huddled around a small propane-fueled camping stove and prepared dinner. The smell of a soup spread throughout our tent as it heated up on the stove. The first bite scalded my tongue and my limbs slowly thawed out as the snow piled up against the sides of the tent.

The next morning, I lay quietly in the warmth of my sleeping bag. The blizzard had stopped sometime in the night and now snow softly swished against the tent, the only sound in the valley. Curious, I sat up and leaned toward the door, unzipping it. I peered through the tent door, looking out at the unblemished snow—even our footsteps were erased overnight.

A quick conference over breakfast decided that the avalanche danger was too high to continue, and the best choice was to go back. We bundled ourselves back into our snow gear, broke down our camp, and swung our backpacks over our shoulders. I clipped myself into my skis and smoothly found my balance as we followed the tree line at the base of the ridge. Snow was piled precariously on every twig and the faint echo of avalanches could be heard occasionally in the distance. I muffled a shriek as a mass of snow slid off of a pine branch and fell close to my skis. Skirting around the new pile of snow, we continued towards the trailhead.

A smile tugged at the corners of my mouth and I took a deep breath of the sharp winter air. Although we had not reached our destination, I had experienced snow camping for the first time. Despite our struggles, these experiences could not be taken away from me and I emerged from the adventure victorious.

Explanation: The backbone of the outline is visible in this story, but the specific details have helped it to come alive. A traditional introduction isn't included, but the first paragraph still acts to familiarize the readers with the situation and give some background to the characters. The thesis isn't incorporated into this story, but having one during the drafting process has helped prevent the story from straying away from the main point.

Even though this story is mostly focused on the narrator and experiences, a piece of dialogue is included. Dialogue is useful because it brings a sense of immediacy to the story. In this narrative, the only piece of dialogue highlights the turning point of the tale, marking the transition from the growing sense of unease (traveling into the wilderness) to the growing sense of satisfaction (traveling out of the wilderness). The last paragraph acts as a conclusion, wrapping up the main ideas and reinforcing the responses to the prompt.

5. Add transitions between the different events.

Read through and make sure the entire narrative flows well. As you change topics, time periods or perspectives, it is important to include transitions so the audience is not lost. If you are describing several different subjects or events, make sure that their relation to each other is clear and logical (see Example Throughout the Process transitions in Box 12.5).

Make sure the passage of time is clear, as well. Adding phrases such as "immediately after," "three hours later" or "after what seemed to be an eternity, but was actually five minutes" can help establish how time relates to the events in your story. There is more specific information on writing transitions in Appendix V. Remember, there should be a distinct impression of flow, as the reader is carried from the beginning of the narration to the end.

Box 12.5: Example Throughout the Process

Examples of Transitions Added to Improve Flow:

Transition 1: *We continued for over an hour, snow dusting* my lashes and turning to small drops of water from the heat radiating off my skin.

Explanation: This new, italicized transition was added to indicate the passage of time. Without this transition, it would be difficult to know how much time had been spent hiking into the mountains. Transitions are not just located at the beginning or end of paragraphs, as you may have seen previously—this one is in the middle of a paragraph. Transitions merely serve to connect different ideas and show the relationship between different points.

Transition 2: I moved carefully, sliding back with every step despite the skins.

My next step let loose a miniature slide of snow. As we froze, a buildup of loose snow began to move as one mass down the mountain and crashed against a thick tree trunk. My friend turned towards me and inclined his head back down the way we had come.

Explanation: This new transition is important because it connects two ideas: struggling up the ridge and the ensuing avalanche. This emphasizes the cause-and-effect relationship between the actions and heightens the tension.

Peer Review

This is a good point for a peer review because the first draft is now complete. When working with personal experiences, it is easy to lose perspective and not realize if something wouldn't make sense to an outside reader. Gaining another point of view through a peer review is vital to make sure the main ideas of the narrative are in place. The peer review should primarily focus on content, focus, organization and flow. Finish all the revisions to the content and overall structure of your paper before you turn your attention to grammar and formatting.

6. Follow Chapters 10 and 11.

From this point onward, the grammar-editing and formatting processes of a narrative essay are similar to other types of papers. As this is a narrative, a casual tone may be appropriate. This means that using contractions, first and second person and colloquial language may help create a desired voice. However, it is still important to maintain clarity.

When referring to Chapter 10: Grammar, focus on Steps 4 through 8. Concentrate especially on Step 8, "Describe using your senses," which contains useful tips for creating a narrative that sparks. After the essay itself is complete and edited, refer to Chapter 11: Formatting. For applying the next steps to the Example Throughout the Process essay, refer to Box 12.6.

Box 12.6: Example Throughout the Process

The final version of this essay can be found in Appendix III. To polish up this narrative, I focused on my word choices, trying to make them as evocative and active as possible. For example, in the second paragraph I changed "pieces of snow" to "flakes of snow" for a more specific word choice.

I also looked at my adjective use. By default, most people tend to use similar, general adjectives time and time again; this is something that I notice quite a bit in my own writing. However, if you slowly look through your paper and pay attention only to the adjectives then you can see patterns and try to replace dull words with more precise ones. For example, when describing dinner in the tent, I replaced "the smell of soup" with "the savory aroma of a stew," a much more evocative and sensory-rich phrase. Finally, I checked for descriptions from a variety of

---

senses, following the guidelines in Chapter 10, Rule 8.

While these revisions didn't change the plot, they did noticeably perk up my writing and made the language more attention-grabbing. In a narrative essay, the presentation of your story is vital and these guidelines can help create an engaging tale.

Takeaway Points

- Drafting a thesis will improve the focus of your paper, even if it is not included in the final draft.

- Creating an outline is vital for writing a story with good flow and organization.

- Transitions show the relationships between different events.

- Describing scenes as specific and vivid as possible will grab the readers' attention and will help them relate to your narrative.

Final Thoughts

The purpose of an academic paper is to answer a prompt. By breaking down a given prompt, you can make sure you are accurately responding to all its facets. To effectively answer any prompt, no matter what it is, the paper must be focused. This is the purpose of a thesis — to provide and demonstrate focus for the paper.

If all parts of your paper support your thesis, and the thesis logically responds to the prompt, then your paper will be respectable. The rest of the process, from writing an introduction to correcting grammar, serves to transition your paper from a solid foundation to an elegant response.

By following the steps in this book, you never need to be stumped by a blank page as you try to pour out a beautiful essay on the first draft. You will never have to face that gut-wrenching realization that your impeccably-written essay does not respond to the prompt, or that half of your paper does not relate to your thesis. These steps will efficiently lead you from brainstorming to a finished product; your paper will always respond to the prompt, have a thesis and be logically written. You have the tools, now go and write!

Appendices

Appendix I: "To Build a Fire"

Here is the full text to Jack London's "To Build a Fire," the short story from which all the "Examples Throughout the Process" are based.

To Build a Fire
by Jack London

Day had broken cold and grey, exceedingly cold and grey, when the man turned aside from the main Yukon trail and climbed the high earth- bank, where a dim and little-travelled trail led eastward through the fat spruce timberland. It was a steep bank, and he paused for breath at the top, excusing the act to himself by looking at his watch. It was nine o'clock. There was no sun nor hint of sun, though there was not a cloud in the sky. It was a clear day, and yet there seemed an intangible pall over the face of things, a subtle gloom that made the day dark, and that was due to the absence of sun. This fact did not worry the man. He was used to the lack of sun. It had been days since he had seen the sun, and he knew that a few more days must pass before that cheerful orb, due south, would just peep above the sky- line and dip immediately from view.

The man flung a look back along the way he had come. The Yukon lay a mile wide and hidden under three feet of ice. On top of this ice were as many feet of snow. It was all pure white, rolling in gentle undulations where the ice-jams of the freeze-up had formed. North and south, as far as his eye could see, it was unbroken white, save for a dark hair-line that curved and twisted from around the spruce- covered island to the south, and that curved and twisted away into the north, where it disappeared behind another spruce-covered island. This dark hair-line was the trail—the main trail—that led south five hundred miles to the Chilcoot Pass, Dyea, and salt water; and that led north seventy miles to Dawson, and still on to the north a thousand miles to Nulato, and finally to St. Michael on Bering Sea, a thousand miles and half a thousand more.

But all this—the mysterious, far-reaching hairline trail, the absence of sun from the sky, the tremendous cold, and the strangeness and weirdness of it all—made no impression on the man. It was not because he was long used to it. He was a new-comer in the land, a chechaquo, and this was his first winter. The trouble with him was that he was without imagination. He was quick and alert in the things of life, but only in the things, and not in the significances. Fifty degrees below zero meant eighty odd degrees of frost. Such fact impressed him as being cold and uncomfortable, and that was all. It did not lead him to meditate upon his frailty as a creature of temperature, and upon man's frailty in general, able only to live within certain narrow limits of heat and cold; and from there on it did not lead him to the conjectural field of immortality and man's place in the universe. Fifty degrees below zero stood for a bite of frost that hurt and that must be guarded against by the use of mittens, ear-flaps, warm moccasins, and thick socks. Fifty degrees below zero was to him just precisely fifty degrees below zero. That there should be anything more to it than that was a thought that never entered his head.

As he turned to go on, he spat speculatively. There was a sharp, explosive crackle that startled him. He spat again. And again, in the air, before it could fall to the snow, the spittle crackled. He knew that at fifty below spittle crackled on the snow, but this spittle had crackled in the air. Undoubtedly it was colder than fifty below — how much colder he did not know. But the temperature did not matter. He was bound for the old claim on the left fork of Henderson Creek, where the boys were already. They had come over across the divide from the Indian Creek country, while he had come the roundabout way to take a look at the possibilities of getting out logs in the spring from the islands in the Yukon. He would be in to camp by six o'clock; a bit after dark, it was true, but the boys would be there, a fire would be going, and a hot supper would be ready. As for lunch, he pressed his hand against the protruding bundle under his jacket. It was also under his shirt, wrapped up in a handkerchief and lying against the naked skin. It was the only way to keep the biscuits from freezing. He smiled agreeably to himself as he thought of those biscuits, each cut open and sopped in bacon grease, and each enclosing a generous slice of fried bacon.

He plunged in among the big spruce trees. The trail was faint. A foot of snow had fallen since the last sled had passed over, and he was glad he was without a sled, travelling light. In fact, he carried nothing but the lunch wrapped in the handkerchief. He was surprised, however, at the cold. It certainly was cold, he concluded, as he rubbed his numbed nose and cheek-bones with his mittened hand. He was a warm-whiskered man, but the hair on his face did not protect the high cheek-bones and the eager nose that thrust itself aggressively into the frosty air.

At the man's heels trotted a dog, a big native husky, the proper wolf-dog, grey-coated and without any visible or temperamental difference from its brother, the wild wolf. The animal was depressed by the tremendous cold. It knew that it was no time for travelling. Its instinct told it a truer tale than was told to the man by the man's judgment. In reality, it was not merely colder than fifty below zero; it was colder than sixty below, than seventy below. It was seventy-five below zero. Since the freezing-point is thirty-two above zero, it meant that one hundred and seven degrees of frost obtained. The dog did not know anything about thermometers. Possibly in its brain there was no sharp consciousness of a condition of very cold such as was in the man's brain. But the brute had its instinct. It experienced a vague but menacing apprehension that subdued it and made it slink along at the man's heels, and that made it question eagerly every unwonted movement of the man as if expecting him to go into camp or to seek shelter somewhere and build a fire. The dog had learned fire, and it wanted fire, or else to burrow under the snow and cuddle its warmth away from the air.

The frozen moisture of its breathing had settled on its fur in a fine powder of frost, and especially were its jowls, muzzle, and eyelashes whitened by its crystalled breath. The man's red beard and moustache were likewise frosted, but more solidly, the deposit taking the form of ice and increasing with every warm, moist breath he exhaled. Also, the man was chewing tobacco, and the muzzle of ice held his lips so rigidly that he was unable to clear his chin when he expelled the juice. The result was that a crystal beard of the colour and solidity of amber was increasing its length on his chin. If he fell down it would shatter itself, like glass, into brittle fragments. But he did not mind the appendage. It was the penalty all tobacco- chewers paid in that country, and he had been out before in two cold snaps. They had not been so cold as this, he knew, but by the spirit thermometer at Sixty Mile he knew they had been registered at fifty below and at fifty-five.

He held on through the level stretch of woods for several miles, crossed a wide flat of nigger-heads, and dropped down a bank to the frozen bed of a small stream. This was Henderson Creek, and he knew he was ten miles from the forks. He looked at his watch. It was ten o'clock. He was making four miles an hour, and he calculated that he would arrive at the forks at half-past twelve. He decided to celebrate that event by eating his lunch there.

The dog dropped in again at his heels, with a tail drooping discouragement, as the man swung along the creek-bed. The furrow of the old sled-trail was plainly visible, but a dozen inches of snow covered the marks of the last runners. In a month no man had come up or down that silent creek. The man held steadily on. He was not much given to thinking, and just then particularly he had nothing to think about save that he would eat lunch at the forks and that at six o'clock he would be in camp with the boys. There was nobody to talk to and, had there been, speech would have been impossible because of the ice-muzzle on his mouth. So he continued monotonously to chew tobacco and to increase the length of his amber beard.

Once in a while the thought reiterated itself that it was very cold and that he had never experienced such cold. As he walked along he rubbed his cheek-bones and nose with the back of his mittened hand. He did this automatically, now and again changing hands. But rub as he would, the instant he stopped his cheek-bones went numb, and the following instant the end of his nose went numb. He was sure to frost his cheeks; he knew that, and experienced a pang of regret that he had not devised a nose-strap of the sort Bud wore in cold snaps. Such a strap passed across the cheeks, as well, and saved them. But it didn't matter much, after all. What were frosted cheeks? A bit painful, that was all; they were never serious.

Empty as the man's mind was of thoughts, he was keenly observant, and he noticed the changes in the creek, the curves and bends and timber- jams, and always he sharply noted where he placed his feet. Once, coming around a bend, he shied abruptly, like a startled horse, curved away from the place where he had been walking, and retreated several paces back along the trail. The creek he knew was frozen clear to the bottom—no creek could contain water in that arctic winter—but he knew also that there were springs that bubbled out from the hillsides and ran along under the snow and on top the ice of the creek. He knew that the coldest snaps never froze these springs, and he knew likewise their danger. They were traps. They hid pools of water under the snow that might be three inches deep, or three feet. Sometimes a skin of ice half an inch thick covered them, and in turn was covered by the snow. Sometimes there were alternate layers of water and ice-skin, so that when one broke through he kept on breaking through for a while, sometimes wetting himself to the waist.

That was why he had shied in such panic. He had felt the give under his feet and heard the crackle of a snow-hidden ice-skin. And to get his feet wet in such a temperature meant trouble and danger. At the very least it meant delay, for he would be forced to stop and build a fire, and under its protection to bare his feet while he dried his socks and moccasins. He stood and studied the creek-bed and its banks, and decided that the flow of water came from the right. He reflected awhile, rubbing his nose and cheeks, then skirted to the left, stepping gingerly and testing the footing for each step. Once clear of the danger, he took a fresh chew of tobacco and swung along at his four-mile gait.

In the course of the next two hours he came upon several similar traps. Usually the snow above the hidden pools had a sunken, candied appearance that advertised the danger. Once again, however, he had a close call; and once, suspecting danger, he compelled the dog to go on in front. The dog did not want to go. It hung back until the man shoved it forward, and then it went quickly across the white, unbroken surface. Suddenly it broke through, floundered to one side, and got away to firmer footing. It had wet its forefeet and legs, and almost immediately the water that clung to it turned to ice. It made quick efforts to lick the ice off its legs, then dropped down in the snow and began to bite out the ice that had formed between the toes. This was a matter of instinct. To permit the ice to remain would mean sore feet. It did not know this. It merely obeyed the mysterious prompting that arose from the deep crypts of its being. But the man knew, having achieved a judgment on the subject, and he removed the mitten from his right hand and helped tear out the ice- particles. He did not expose his fingers more than a minute, and was astonished at the swift numbness that smote them. It certainly was cold. He pulled on the mitten hastily, and beat the hand savagely across his chest.

At twelve o'clock the day was at its brightest. Yet the sun was too far south on its winter journey to clear the horizon. The bulge of the earth intervened between it and Henderson Creek, where the man walked under a clear sky at noon and cast no shadow. At half-past twelve, to the minute, he arrived at the forks of the creek. He was pleased at the speed he had made. If he kept it up, he would certainly be with the boys by six. He unbuttoned his jacket and shirt and drew forth his lunch. The action consumed no more than a quarter of a minute, yet in that brief moment the numbness laid hold of the exposed fingers. He did not put the mitten on, but, instead, struck the fingers a dozen sharp smashes against his leg. Then he sat down on a snow-covered log to eat. The sting that followed upon the striking of his fingers against his leg ceased so quickly that he was startled, he had had no chance to take a bite of biscuit. He struck the fingers repeatedly and returned them to the mitten, baring the other hand for the purpose of eating. He tried to take a mouthful, but the ice-muzzle prevented. He had forgotten to build a fire and thaw out. He chuckled at his foolishness, and as he chuckled he noted the numbness creeping into the exposed fingers. Also, he noted that the stinging which had first come to his toes when he sat down was already passing away. He wondered whether the toes were warm or numbed. He moved them inside the moccasins and decided that they were numbed.

He pulled the mitten on hurriedly and stood up. He was a bit frightened. He stamped up and down until the stinging returned into the feet. It certainly was cold, was his thought. That man from Sulphur Creek had spoken the truth when telling how cold it sometimes got in the country. And he had laughed at him at the time! That showed one must not be too sure of things. There was no mistake about it, it was cold. He strode up and down, stamping his feet and threshing his arms, until reassured by the returning warmth. Then he got out matches and proceeded to make a fire. From the undergrowth, where high water of the previous spring had lodged a supply of seasoned twigs, he got his firewood. Working carefully from a small beginning, he soon had a roaring fire, over which he thawed the ice from his face and in the protection of which he ate his biscuits. For the moment the cold of space was outwitted. The dog took satisfaction in the fire, stretching out close enough for warmth and far enough away to escape being singed.

When the man had finished, he filled his pipe and took his comfortable time over a smoke. Then he pulled on his mittens, settled the ear-flaps of his cap firmly about his ears, and took the creek trail up the left fork. The dog was disappointed and yearned back toward the fire. This man did not know cold. Possibly all the generations of his ancestry had been ignorant of cold, of real cold, of cold one hundred and seven degrees below freezing-point. But the dog knew; all its ancestry knew, and it had inherited the knowledge. And it knew that it was not good to walk abroad in such fearful cold. It was the time to lie snug in a hole in the snow and wait for a curtain of cloud to be drawn across the face of outer space whence this cold came. On the other hand, there was keen intimacy between the dog and the man. The one was the toil-slave of the other, and the only caresses it had ever received were the caresses of the whip-lash and of harsh and menacing throat-sounds that threatened the whip-lash. So the dog made no effort to communicate its apprehension to the man. It was not concerned in the welfare of the man; it was for its own sake that it yearned back toward the fire. But the man whistled, and spoke to it with the sound of whip-lashes, and the dog swung in at the man's heels and followed after.

The man took a chew of tobacco and proceeded to start a new amber beard. Also, his moist breath quickly powdered with white his moustache, eyebrows, and lashes. There did not seem to be so many springs on the left fork of the Henderson, and for half an hour the man saw no signs of any. And then it happened. At a place where there were no signs, where the soft, unbroken snow seemed to advertise solidity beneath, the man broke through. It was not deep. He wetted himself half-way to the knees before he floundered out to the firm crust.

He was angry, and cursed his luck aloud. He had hoped to get into camp with the boys at six o'clock, and this would delay him an hour, for he would have to build a fire and dry out his foot-gear. This was imperative at that low temperature—he knew that much; and he turned aside to the bank, which he climbed. On top, tangled in the underbrush about the trunks of several small spruce trees, was a high-water deposit of dry firewood—sticks and twigs principally, but also larger portions of seasoned branches and fine, dry, last-year's grasses. He threw down several large pieces on top of the snow. This served for a foundation and prevented the young flame from drowning itself in the snow it otherwise would melt. The flame he got by touching a match to a small shred of birch-bark that he took from his pocket. This burned even more readily than paper. Placing it on the foundation, he fed the young flame with wisps of dry grass and with the tiniest dry twigs.

He worked slowly and carefully, keenly aware of his danger. Gradually, as the flame grew stronger, he increased the size of the twigs with which he fed it. He squatted in the snow, pulling the twigs out from their entanglement in the brush and feeding directly to the flame. He knew there must be no failure. When it is seventy- five below zero, a man must not fail in his first attempt to build a fire—that is, if his feet are wet. If his feet are dry, and he fails, he can run along the trail for half a mile and restore his circulation. But the circulation of wet and freezing feet cannot be restored by running when it is seventy-five below. No matter how fast he runs, the wet feet will freeze the harder.

All this the man knew. The old-timer on Sulphur Creek had told him about it the previous fall, and now he was appreciating the advice. Already all sensation had gone out of his feet. To build the fire he had been forced to remove his mittens, and the fingers had quickly gone numb. His pace of four miles an hour had kept his heart pumping blood to the surface of his body and to all the extremities. But the instant he stopped, the action of the pump eased down. The cold of space smote the unprotected tip of the planet, and he, being on that unprotected tip, received the full force of the blow. The blood of his body recoiled before it. The blood was alive, like the dog, and like the dog it wanted to hide away and cover itself up from the fearful cold. So long as he walked four miles an hour, he pumped that blood, willy-nilly, to the surface; but now it ebbed away and sank down into the recesses of his body. The extremities were the first to feel its absence. His wet feet froze the faster, and his exposed fingers numbed the faster, though they had not yet begun to freeze. Nose and cheeks were already freezing, while the skin of all his body chilled as it lost its blood.

But he was safe. Toes and nose and cheeks would be only touched by the frost, for the fire was beginning to burn with strength. He was feeding it with twigs the size of his finger. In another minute he would be able to feed it with branches the size of his wrist, and then he could remove his wet foot-gear, and, while it dried, he could keep his naked feet warm by the fire, rubbing them at first, of course, with snow. The fire was a success. He was safe. He remembered the advice of the old-timer on Sulphur Creek, and smiled. The old-timer had been very serious in laying down the law that no man must travel alone in the Klondike after fifty below. Well, here he was; he had had the accident; he was alone; and he had saved himself. Those old-timers were rather womanish, some of them, he thought. All a man had to do was to keep his head, and he was all right. Any man who was a man could travel alone. But it was surprising, the rapidity with which his cheeks and nose were freezing. And he had not thought his fingers could go lifeless in so short a time. Lifeless they were, for he could scarcely make them move together to grip a twig, and they seemed remote from his body and from him. When he touched a twig, he had to look and see whether or not he had hold of it. The wires were pretty well down between him and his finger-ends.

All of which counted for little. There was the fire, snapping and crackling and promising life with every dancing flame. He started to untie his moccasins. They were coated with ice; the thick German socks were like sheaths of iron half-way to the knees; and the mocassin strings were like rods of steel all twisted and knotted as by some conflagration. For a moment he tugged with his numbed fingers, then, realizing the folly of it, he drew his sheath-knife.

But before he could cut the strings, it happened. It was his own fault or, rather, his mistake. He should not have built the fire under the spruce tree. He should have built it in the open. But it had been easier to pull the twigs from the brush and drop them directly on the fire. Now the tree under which he had done this carried a weight of snow on its boughs. No wind had blown for weeks, and each bough was fully freighted. Each time he had pulled a twig he had communicated a slight agitation to the tree—an imperceptible agitation, so far as he was concerned, but an agitation sufficient to bring about the disaster. High up in the tree one bough capsized its load of snow. This fell on the boughs beneath, capsizing them. This process continued, spreading out and involving the whole tree. It grew like an avalanche, and it descended without warning upon the man and the fire, and the fire was blotted out! Where it had burned was a mantle of fresh and disordered snow.

The man was shocked. It was as though he had just heard his own sentence of death. For a moment he sat and stared at the spot where the fire had been. Then he grew very calm. Perhaps the old-timer on Sulphur Creek was right. If he had only had a trail-mate he would have been in no danger now. The trail-mate could have built the fire. Well, it was up to him to build the fire over again, and this second time there must be no failure. Even if he succeeded, he would most likely lose some toes. His feet must be badly frozen by now, and there would be some time before the second fire was ready.

Such were his thoughts, but he did not sit and think them. He was busy all the time they were passing through his mind, he made a new foundation for a fire, this time in the open; where no treacherous tree could blot it out. Next, he gathered dry grasses and tiny twigs from the high-water flotsam. He could not bring his fingers together to pull them out, but he was able to gather them by the handful. In this way he got many rotten twigs and bits of green moss that were undesirable, but it was the best he could do. He worked methodically, even collecting an armful of the larger branches to be used later when the fire gathered strength. And all the while the dog sat and watched him, a certain yearning wistfulness in its eyes, for it looked upon him as the fire-provider, and the fire was slow in coming.

When all was ready, the man reached in his pocket for a second piece of birch-bark. He knew the bark was there, and, though he could not feel it with his fingers, he could hear its crisp rustling as he fumbled for it. Try as he would, he could not clutch hold of it. And all the time, in his consciousness, was the knowledge that each instant his feet were freezing. This thought tended to put him in a panic, but he fought against it and kept calm. He pulled on his mittens with his teeth, and threshed his arms back and forth, beating his hands with all his might against his sides. He did this sitting down, and he stood up to do it; and all the while the dog sat in the snow, its wolf-brush of a tail curled around warmly over its forefeet, its sharp wolf-ears pricked forward intently as it watched the man. And the man as he beat and threshed with his arms and hands, felt a great surge of envy as he regarded the creature that was warm and secure in its natural covering.

After a time he was aware of the first far-away signals of sensation in his beaten fingers. The faint tingling grew stronger till it evolved into a stinging ache that was excruciating, but which the man hailed with satisfaction. He stripped the mitten from his right hand and fetched forth the birch-bark. The exposed fingers were quickly going numb again. Next he brought out his bunch of sulphur matches. But the tremendous cold had already driven the life out of his fingers. In his effort to separate one match from the others, the whole bunch fell in the snow. He tried to pick it out of the snow, but failed. The dead fingers could neither touch nor clutch. He was very careful. He drove the thought of his freezing feet; and nose, and cheeks, out of his mind, devoting his whole soul to the matches. He watched, using the sense of vision in place of that of touch, and when he saw his fingers on each side the bunch, he closed them—that is, he willed to close them, for the wires were drawn, and the fingers did not obey. He pulled the mitten on the right hand, and beat it fiercely against his knee. Then, with both mittened hands, he scooped the bunch of matches, along with much snow, into his lap. Yet he was no better off.

After some manipulation he managed to get the bunch between the heels of his mittened hands. In this fashion he carried it to his mouth. The ice crackled and snapped when by a violent effort he opened his mouth. He drew the lower jaw in, curled the upper lip out of the way, and scraped the bunch with his upper teeth in order to separate a match. He succeeded in getting one, which he dropped on his lap. He was no better off. He could not pick it up. Then he devised a way. He picked it up in his teeth and scratched it on his leg. Twenty times he scratched before he succeeded in lighting it. As it flamed he held it with his teeth to the birch-bark. But the burning brimstone went up his nostrils and into his lungs, causing him to cough spasmodically. The match fell into the snow and went out.

The old-timer on Sulphur Creek was right, he thought in the moment of controlled despair that ensued:

after fifty below, a man should travel with a partner. He beat his hands, but failed in exciting any sensation. Suddenly he bared both hands, removing the mittens with his teeth. He caught the whole bunch between the heels of his hands. His arm-muscles not being frozen enabled him to press the hand-heels tightly against the matches. Then he scratched the bunch along his leg. It flared into flame, seventy sulphur matches at once! There was no wind to blow them out. He kept his head to one side to escape the strangling fumes, and held the blazing bunch to the birch-bark. As he so held it, he became aware of sensation in his hand. His flesh was burning. He could smell it. Deep down below the surface he could feel it. The sensation developed into pain that grew acute. And still he endured it, holding the flame of the matches clumsily to the bark that would not light readily because his own burning hands were in the way, absorbing most of the flame.

At last, when he could endure no more, he jerked his hands apart. The blazing matches fell sizzling into the snow, but the birch-bark was alight. He began laying dry grasses and the tiniest twigs on the flame. He could not pick and choose, for he had to lift the fuel between the heels of his hands. Small pieces of rotten wood and green moss clung to the twigs, and he bit them off as well as he could with his teeth. He cherished the flame carefully and awkwardly. It meant life, and it must not perish. The withdrawal of blood from the surface of his body now made him begin to shiver, and he grew more awkward. A large piece of green moss fell squarely on the little fire. He tried to poke it out with his fingers, but his shivering frame made him poke too far, and he disrupted the nucleus of the little fire, the burning grasses and tiny twigs separating and scattering. He tried to poke them together again, but in spite of the tenseness of the effort, his shivering got away with him, and the twigs were hopelessly scattered. Each twig gushed a puff of smoke and went out. The fire-provider had failed. As he looked apathetically about him, his eyes chanced on the dog, sitting across the ruins of the fire from him, in the snow, making restless, hunching movements, slightly lifting one forefoot and then the other, shifting its weight back and forth on them with wistful eagerness.

The sight of the dog put a wild idea into his head. He remembered the tale of the man, caught in a blizzard, who killed a steer and crawled inside the carcass, and so was saved. He would kill the dog and bury his hands in the warm body until the numbness went out of them. Then he could build another fire. He spoke to the dog, calling it to him; but in his voice was a strange note of fear that frightened the animal, who had never known the man to speak in such way before. Something was the matter, and its suspicious nature sensed danger,—it knew not what danger but somewhere, somehow, in its brain arose an apprehension of the man. It flattened its ears down at the sound of the man's voice, and its restless, hunching movements and the liftings and shiftings of its forefeet became more pronounced but it would not come to the man. He got on his hands and knees and crawled toward the dog. This unusual posture again excited suspicion, and the animal sidled mincingly away.

The man sat up in the snow for a moment and struggled for calmness. Then he pulled on his mittens, by means of his teeth, and got upon his feet. He glanced down at first in order to assure himself that he was really standing up, for the absence of sensation in his feet left him unrelated to the earth. His erect position in itself started to drive the webs of suspicion from the dog's mind; and when he spoke peremptorily, with the sound of whip-lashes in his voice, the dog rendered its customary allegiance and came to him. As it came within reaching distance, the man lost his control. His arms flashed out to the dog, and he experienced genuine surprise when he discovered that his hands could not clutch, that there was neither bend nor feeling in the lingers. He had forgotten for the moment that they were frozen and that they were freezing more and more. All this happened quickly, and before the animal could get away, he encircled its body with his arms. He sat down in the snow, and in this fashion held the dog, while it snarled and whined and struggled.

But it was all he could do, hold its body encircled in his arms and sit there. He realized that he could not kill the dog. There was no way to do it. With his helpless hands he could neither draw nor hold his sheath-knife nor throttle the animal. He released it, and it plunged wildly away, with tail between its legs, and still snarling. It halted forty feet away and surveyed him curiously, with ears sharply pricked forward. The man looked down at his hands in order to locate them, and found them hanging on the ends of his arms. It struck him as curious that one should have to use his eyes in order to find out where his hands were. He began threshing his arms back and forth, beating the mittened hands against his sides. He did this for five minutes, violently, and his heart pumped enough blood up to the surface to put a stop to his shivering. But no sensation was aroused in the hands. He had an impression that they hung like weights on the ends of his arms, but when he tried to run the impression down, he could not find it.

A certain fear of death, dull and oppressive, came to him. This fear quickly became poignant as he realized that it was no longer a mere matter of freezing his fingers and toes, or of losing his hands and feet, but that it was a matter of life and death with the chances against him. This threw him into a panic, and he turned and ran up the creek-bed along the old, dim trail. The dog joined in behind and kept up with him. He ran blindly, without intention, in fear such as he had never known in his life. Slowly, as he ploughed and floundered through the snow, he began to see things again—the banks of the creek, the old timber-jams, the leafless aspens, and the sky. The running made him feel better. He did not shiver. Maybe, if he ran on, his feet would thaw out; and, anyway, if he ran far enough, he would reach camp and the boys. Without doubt he would lose some fingers and toes and some of his face; but the boys would take care of him, and save the rest of him when he got there. And at the same time there was another thought in his mind that said he would never get to the camp and the boys; that it was too many miles away, that the freezing had too great a start on him, and that he would soon be stiff and dead. This thought he kept in the background and refused to consider. Sometimes it pushed itself forward and demanded to be heard, but he thrust it back and strove to think of other things.

It struck him as curious that he could run at all on feet so frozen that he could not feel them when they struck the earth and took the weight of his body. He seemed to himself to skim along above the surface and to have no connection with the earth. Somewhere he had once seen a winged Mercury, and he wondered if Mercury felt as he felt when skimming over the earth.

His theory of running until he reached camp and the boys had one flaw in it: he lacked the endurance. Several times he stumbled, and finally he tottered, crumpled up, and fell. When he tried to rise, he failed. He must sit and rest, he decided, and next time he would merely walk and keep on going. As he sat and regained his breath, he noted that he was feeling quite warm and comfortable. He was not shivering, and it even seemed that a warm glow had come to his chest and trunk. And yet, when he touched his nose or cheeks, there was no sensation. Running would not thaw them out. Nor would it thaw out his hands and feet. Then the thought came to him that the frozen portions of his body must be extending. He tried to keep this thought down, to forget it, to think of something else; he was aware of the panicky feeling that it caused, and he was afraid of the panic. But the thought asserted itself, and persisted, until it produced a vision of his body totally frozen. This was too much, and he made another wild run along the trail. Once he slowed down to a walk, but the thought of the freezing extending itself made him run again.

And all the time the dog ran with him, at his heels. When he fell down a second time, it curled its tail over its forefeet and sat in front of him facing him curiously eager and intent. The warmth and security of the animal angered him, and he cursed it till it flattened down its ears appeasingly. This time the shivering came more quickly upon the man. He was losing in his battle with the frost. It was creeping into his body from all sides. The thought of it drove him on, but he ran no more than a hundred feet, when he staggered and pitched headlong. It was his last panic. When he had recovered his breath and control, he sat up and entertained in his mind the conception of meeting death with dignity. However, the conception did not come to him in such terms. His idea of it was that he had been making a fool of himself, running around like a chicken with its head cut off—such was the simile that occurred to him. Well, he was bound to freeze anyway, and he might as well take it decently. With this new-found peace of mind came the first glimmerings of drowsiness. A good idea, he thought, to sleep off to death. It was like taking an anaesthetic. Freezing was not so bad as people thought. There were lots worse ways to die.

He pictured the boys finding his body next day. Suddenly he found himself with them, coming along the trail and looking for himself. And, still with them, he came around a turn in the trail and found himself lying in the snow. He did not belong with himself any more, for even then he was out of himself, standing with the boys and looking at himself in the snow. It certainly was cold, was his thought. When he got back to the States he could tell the folks what real cold was. He drifted on from this to a vision of the old-timer on Sulphur Creek. He could see him quite clearly, warm and comfortable, and smoking a pipe.

"You were right, old hoss; you were right," the man mumbled to the old-timer of Sulphur Creek.

Then the man drowsed off into what seemed to him the most comfortable and satisfying sleep he had ever known. The dog sat facing him and waiting. The brief day drew to a close in a long, slow twilight. There were no signs of a fire to be made, and, besides, never in the dog's experience had it known a man to sit like that in the snow and make no fire. As the twilight drew on, its eager yearning for the fire mastered it, and with a great lifting and shifting of forefeet, it whined softly, then flattened its ears down in anticipation of being chidden by the man. But the man remained silent. Later, the dog whined loudly. And still later it crept close to the man and caught the scent of death. This made the animal bristle and back away. A little longer it delayed, howling under the stars that leaped and danced and shone brightly in the cold sky. Then it turned and trotted up the trail in the direction of the camp it knew, where were the other food-providers and fire-providers.

Appendix II: A Persuasive Essay

This is the final draft of the persuasive essay created in the Example Throughout the Process sections. Each of the steps has been broken down and explained in Chapters 1 through 8; here is the culmination, with all the pieces assembled into a final essay. As this is a persuasive essay, the emphasis is placed on a strong, opinionated thesis statement supported by specific concrete details, with commentary providing the necessary link between the two.

The Benefits of Looking Ahead

The snow crunched under my feet, flakes hitting my face and leaving behind small droplets. Taking a deep breath, I inhaled the sharp smell of pine. This weekend was my first time snow camping and I ran through everything I needed once again, checking it mentally against the items in my pack. While I had planned extensively for my trip and ran into few troubles, the protagonist in Jack London's short story "To Build a Fire" faced much more dire circumstances and consequences. Jack London was an American author who lived at the end of the nineteenth century and the beginning of the twentieth century. In 1897, he joined the Klondike Gold Rush, also known as the Yukon Gold Rush, looking for gold in the Klondike area of Canada (Streissguth). London's famous short story "To Build a Fire" tells the tale of a nameless man who decides to travel by himself through the Yukon in frigid temperatures. With only his dog for company, he ignores the advice of other men in town to never travel alone and falls through ice to a stream beneath, drenching his legs. Without a companion to help him, he fails at making a successful fire to dry himself and he freezes to death. Jack London's "To Build a Fire" presents the protagonist's final downfall as his failure to assess the repercussions of his own decisions, including his lack of appreciation of elemental hazards, his failure to build fire and his insistence on traveling alone.

Despite the extremely cold temperatures, the protagonist does not extend that information to foresee potential harm to himself. When introducing the protagonist, the narrator relates that "Fifty degrees below zero was to him just precisely fifty degrees below zero...That there should be anything more to it than that was a thought that never entered his head" (London). The words "just precisely" imply that the temperature is only a temperature to the Man, nothing more and nothing less. He decides to venture out into this cold weather without thinking of any effects the temperature might have on his journey—in fact, this thought "never entered his head." It is very telling that the character, who is about to enter a wild and untamed land alone, does not even consider the temperature to have any effect on his trip. At the beginning of the Man's journey, he spits in the cold air and there is "a sharp, explosive crackle that startled him," but he did not think any more of it (London). "Sharp" and "explosive" are harsh and staccato words that imply violence, and the noise, due to the intense cold, surprises the Man. However, he fails to make any cognitive link between the violence implied in the unexpected sound and potential violence to himself. After the Man starts traveling, his cheeks and nose begin to frost and he has a "pang of regret that he had not devised a nose-strap of the sort Bud wore in cold snaps" (London). Early in his trip, the Man experiences an immediate consequence to the frigid temperatures, but this still does not cause him to draw any further conclusions about the intense cold that he has never before experienced. Furthermore, the regret is only described as a "pang," which suggests a small, unimportant feeling that will soon pass. Despite the fact that he has already experienced unexpected consequences, he still does not see any further repercussions to his decision to travel a long distance in such extreme weather. After the Man falls through ice, this severe weather forces him to stop traveling and immediately try to make fire in order to dry out his wet feet.

Even though the Man knows the delicate nature of a new fire in the snow, he still does not think ahead when he is building his first. During his initial attempt, he knows the importance of preventing the flame from being drowned in snow—this is why he lays down the larger sticks over which he makes his first fire (London). This takes extra effort, especially in the chilling temperatures that are stiffening his fingers, and it is very clear that the Man realizes how fragile a small fire is and how important this fire is to him. However, because of these initial extra effort to protect the fire, it is even more telling that he does not appreciate his precarious location under the snow-laden trees. He builds his fire under a tree heaped with snow, pulling twigs directly from the tree which eventually disturbs the snow, causing it to fall. Each time he pulls a twig off it is "an imperceptible agitation, so far as he was concerned," which leads to the snow falling (London). The phrase "so far as he was concerned" tells the audience that, contrary to his previous statement that the shaking is "imperceptible," he can detect the shaking and just decides that it is not worth caring about. The Man decides to pull twigs off of the trees without linking his actions to the possible fatal effects—the movement may cause the heavy snow to fall on his vulnerable fire. Still, the man is "shocked" at the sudden snow fall that obliterates his chance at survival (London). The word "shocked" reinforces the Man's lack of connection between his multiple risky behaviors and the undesirable outcome. He genuinely does not think through his fire-building efforts and therefore the result comes as a surprise. It is at this point that the Man starts to reflect upon the usefulness a companion could have provided.

Despite being warned against traveling alone, the Man does not realize any danger it implies until he is in dire need of a companion. In response to the cautions of the old men in the town, he says to himself "All a man had to do was keep his head...Any man who was a man could travel alone" (London). The word "all" implies that keeping one's head is the only requirement to staying alive when traveling alone, echoed by the word "any" in the second phrase, leading to the conclusion that this feat is not even extraordinary. These are more than merely boastful statements, but instead demonstrate a critical failure to assess a situation. These statements seem more fitting to an afternoon jaunt and feel very out-of-place for someone about to travel the treacherous Yukon terrain in harsh winter weather, where a misstep could mean a painful death. After the Man fails in his second attempt to build a fire, in despair he thinks to himself that "The old-timer on Sulphur Creek was right...after fifty below, a man should travel with a partner" (London). The phrasing of this sentence shows that even after failing to build his second fire, even when faced with imminent death, the man is still avoiding taking responsibility of his own mistake in not bringing a companion with him. Even when he realizes that a partner is vital in such a harsh environment, his thought still avoids any reference to him being in the wrong. He uses the phrase "the old-timer...was right," instead of using the converse by saying that he, the Man, was wrong. In addition, he uses the detached third person when he states that "a man should travel with a partner." There is still no acceptance of his own mistakes, still no outright connection between his own fault and his current danger.

The protagonist in this story does not make causal connections as he fails time and time again to associate a known risk with any potential ramifications to himself. Despite the temperature being colder than any he had ever felt, he fails even so much as to change what he wears in response to the icy chill. When he attempts to create fire, even though he knows how fragile and important the fire is, he still engages in several risky behaviors without thinking his actions through. Finally, his insistence on traveling alone leaves him no hope of succor. Even at the end of his life he continues to deny his responsibility in choosing not to travel with a companion and the eventual fatal outcome. This demonstrates the crucial importance of thinking decisions through to their consequences. When I turned my face up towards the oncoming mountains, excited for my commencing adventure in snow camping, I was secure that I had planned for possible problems. All decisions have ramifications, however, not merely decisions in a snowy wilderness. Next time you make a choice without considering another option, think—what consequences could there be?

Appendix III: A Narrative Essay

This is the final draft of the narrative essay created in the Example Throughout the Process sections in Chapter 12. This draft has been polished and the word choices have been refined to create strong descriptions around a focused narrative, hallmarks of narrative essays.

Avalanche Danger

The fresh snow squeaked underfoot as my friend and I arrived at the trail-head, where we would start our hike up a snowy valley. This was to be a trip of many firsts: my first time snow camping, my first time hiking on skis, even my first time hiking in the snow. Out of my pack I grabbed my "skins," pieces of specialized material that would be fastened to the bottoms of my skis to prevent me from sliding backwards, making it possible for me to hike uphill in deep snow without sinking up to my waist.

I took a few steps forward on the unwieldy skis, the heavy pack shifting my center of gravity. My friend took off confidently and I trailed behind, skis slipping sideways every few steps. A heavy pine scent hovered in the air and a few flakes of snow touched upon my nose. The snow was laying down a thick blanket over the landscape, muffling every sound. We continued for over an hour, snow dusting my lashes and turning to small drops of water from the heat radiating off my skin. My pace slowed as I saw my friend stopped ahead, peering upwards. He turned towards me as I neared.

"We've lost the trail with all of this snow. We'll have to go over the ridge here."

I nodded, unease curling in my abdomen as I considered the steep incline; I had barely managed to master moving on the nearly flat path. The first few switchbacks were not much more difficult than what we had just traversed, but as twilight fell and the snowfall grew heavy, the path became a near vertical climb. Refusing to admit defeat, our pace slowed to a crawl as we crept up the slope. I moved carefully, sliding back with every movement despite the skins.

My next step let loose a miniature slide of snow. As we froze, a buildup of loose snow below us began to move as one mass down the mountain and crashed against a thick tree trunk. My friend turned towards me and jerked his head back down the way we had come. I nodded grimly—the avalanche danger was too high and we had to turn back after three hours of suffering up the ridge.

We took off our skis to avoid the risks of skiing in dangerous conditions and then half-slid, half-struggled down the hill in waist-deep snow. Spotting a safe spot to make camp among a circle of tall trees, we quickly set up our tent to hide from the blizzard. As the wind whipped the branches far above and the snow lashed against the side of the tent, we huddled around a small propane-fueled camping stove and prepared dinner. The savory aroma of a stew spread throughout our tent as it warmed on the stove. The first bite scalded my tongue; my limbs slowly thawed out as the snow piled up against the sides of the tent.

The next morning, I lay quietly in the warm embrace of my sleeping bag. The blizzard had stopped sometime in the night and now snow softly swished against the tent, the only sound in the valley. Curious, I sat up and leaned toward the door, unzipping it. The metallic whine of the zipper rang out and I peered through the opening, looking out at the unblemished snow—even our footsteps had been erased overnight.

A quick conference over breakfast decided that the avalanche danger was too high to continue and the best choice was to go back. We efficiently bundled ourselves back into our snow gear, broke down our camp, and swung our backpacks over our shoulders. I clipped myself into my skis and smoothly found my balance as we followed the tree line at the base of the ridge. Snow was piled precariously on every twig and the faint echo of avalanches could be heard occasionally in the distance. I muffled a shriek as a mass of snow slid off of a pine branch and crashed an arm's length from my skis. Skirting around the new pile of snow, we continued towards the trailhead.

As our car came into view, a smile tugged at the corners of my mouth and I took a deep breath of the sharp winter air. Although we had not reached our destination, I had experienced snow camping for the first time. Despite our struggles, these experiences could not be taken away from me and I emerged from the adventure, victorious.

Appendix IV: Concrete Details

All Concrete Details Collected for the Persuasive Example Throughout the Process

Thesis: In "To Build a Fire," the Man's ultimate downfall is due to his inability to think ahead and make causal relationships.

Supporting Topic 1: Cold Temperatures
- "Fifty degrees below zero was to him just precisely fifty degrees below zero. That there should be anything more to it than that was a thought that never entered his head."
- "Fifty degrees below zero meant eighty odd degrees of frost. Such fact impressed him as being cold and uncomfortable, and that was all."
- When he spat, "There was a sharp, explosive crackle that startled him" but he did not think any more of it.
- "He was surprised, however, at the cold."
- "muzzle of ice"—the description of what chewing tobacco caused around his mouth. This "muzzle" held the Man's mouth closed and he continued chewing it.
- He had a "pang of regret that he had not devised a nose-strap of the sort Bud wore in cold snaps."

- He "was astonished at the swift numbness that smote them"—his fingers after they had been out for less than a minute

Supporting Topic 2: Lack of a Companion
- "All a man had to do was keep his head."
- "Any man who was a man could travel alone."
- "If he had only had a trail-mate he would have been in no danger now. The trail-mate could have built the fire."
- "The old-timer on Sulphur Creek was right... after fifty below, a man should travel with a partner." He could not build a fire by himself.

Supporting Topic 3: Building a Fire
- He knew the importance of preventing the flame from being drowned in snow—this is why he laid down the larger sticks over which he made his first fire.
- He built his fire under a tree heaped with snow, pulling twigs from the tree which eventually disturbed the snow, causing it to fall. Each time he pulled a twig off it was "an imperceptible agitation, so far as he was concerned," which led to the snow falling.
- Still, the man was "shocked" at the sudden snow fall.
- "His feet must be badly frozen by now, and there would be some time before the second fire was ready."
- "He cherished the flame carefully and awkwardly. It meant life, and it must not perish."
- "The old-timer on Sulphur Creek was right, he thought in the moment of controlled despair that ensued: after fifty below, a man should travel with a partner." (after second fire)

Appendix V: Transition Words

Transitions are needed when there is a topic change; this is often at the beginning or end of a paragraph, but also sometimes when you have multiple concrete details, pieces of commentary, examples or time periods. Including a transition word or phrase can smooth the flow and show how the different topics are related to each other. Keep in mind that there are many more transition words and phrases than those listed here.

Transitions to Continue an Idea:
- Furthermore
- In addition
- Consequently
- Moreover
- Also
- Next

Transitions to Express a Contrary Idea:
- However
- But
- Yet
- On the Contrary
- Nevertheless

Transitions to Show a Change in Time:

- Before
- Previously
- Afterwards
- Then
- After a minute/an hour/a day
- Eventually

Appendix VI: Glossary

Annotated Bibliography: A Works Cited with one to two paragraphs per citation explaining context, significance, and drawbacks of the source.

APA (American Psychological Association): A style of writing and citations common in papers about social science.

Block Quote: A long quotation, usually four lines or longer, used within the text of an essay.

Body Paragraph: A paragraph that upholds and explains the thesis. It usually includes both concrete details and commentary.

Boundary Marker Words: Words in the prompt that define the limits of the paper.

Call to Action: A common device that challenges readers to change or act in some way, usually found in the conclusion.

Chicago Manual of Style: A style of writing common in social science or history papers.

Colloquial Language: Informal words, such as swear words, local descriptive phrases and slang, usually specific to one geographic region.

Commentary: One or more sentences used to show the

significance of a concrete detail and explain in the writer's own words how it supports the thesis.

Compare/Contrast Essay: A type of persuasive essay showing similarities and/or differences between two elements.

Conclusion: The last paragraph(s) in the paper. This wraps up the main ideas presented in the paper.

Concrete Detail: Piece of evidence used as support for your central argument. This may be a fact, a quote, a paraphrase or a summary and must always be cited.

Coupler: A short phrase of the writer's own words which can be placed before or after a concrete detail, helping to improve flow between the piece of evidence and the rest of the paragraph.

Double Spacing: A style of formatting where the lines of text are spread out with the equivalent of one blank line between each line of text.

Fact: A specific piece of evidence that cannot be argued. Examples include statistics, objective statements of events and dates.

First Person: A style of writing where the author refers to him/herself directly using the words "I," "me," "my," "mine," "we," "us," "our" or "ours."

Font: The style of the typeface used.

Footer: Information included in the margin below the text of each page.

Formatting: The visual presentation of a written work on a page.

Free Writing: A method of brainstorming by writing a stream of consciousness in paragraph form without regard to grammar or normal formatting rules.

Full Citation: A complete set of information for a source, usually found in the Works Cited page.

Hanging Indentation: The standard way to format the Works Cited section. The first line of each citation is flush with the left margin, but if the citation continues onto a second or third line then those lines are indented by one half of an inch.

Header: Information included in the margin above the text of each page.

Heading: The important personal, identifying information at the top of the first page of a paper.

Hook: A short section at the beginning of the introduction which is meant to capture the readers' attention.

Idea Web: A method of visual brainstorming where a key word or phrase from the prompt is written in the middle of a piece of paper. Brainstormed points are added "branching" from this central point.

Indentation: A formatting tool where the text starts further to the right than the margin. This is common at the start of a new paragraph, where the first line is further to the right than the rest of the paragraph.

Informative Essay: A paper that objectively tell the readers about a subject.

In-text Citation: A reference that directly following a concrete detail within the text. It signals to the readers that the information is not original to the essay and states which source in the Works Cited this information came from.

Integrated Quote: A short quotation woven into the text of an essay.

Introduction: The first paragraph of the essay, usually presenting background information and the thesis.

Issue Number: The individual number of a journal within a volume.

Journal: An academic periodical which is usually released multiple times a year.

Journal Article: An article, usually peer-reviewed, appearing in an academic publication.

Lead-in: The term for a coupler placed before a concrete detail.

Margin: The white space around the border of a paper.

Medium of Publication: The manner in which the work was released, often "print," "web," or "e-book."

MLA (Modern Language Association): A common writing style used most often in language arts papers.

Narrative Essay: A paper that tells a story.

Outline: An organized presentation of the main points of a paper.

Parallel Grammatical Structure: A method of balancing multiple clauses with similar grammatical structure in a sentence.

Paraphrase: A type of concrete detail where an author accurately rephrases, in his/her own words, a passage from another work. The paraphrase should be a similar length to the original phrase or passage.

Peer Review: The process of having another person give feedback on an essay.

Periodical: Another term for an academic journal, so named because these types of journals are released "periodically."

Persuasive Essay: A paper whose purpose is to convince the readers to one point of view.

Prompt: The topic the paper is meant to be about or the question the writer is meant to answer.

Pronouns: Words used to replace nouns. Pronouns include "I," "you," "he," "she," "it," "we" and "they."

Quantity Words: Words implying a specific number, such as *"one* article" or *"several* articles." These words are important to note when decoding a prompt.

Quote: The exact re-statement of a passage from the source material, usually surrounded by quotation marks.

Resources: The sources of concrete details for an essay.

Rhetorical Question: A question posed that does not need a literal answer.

Second Person: A style of writing where the author refers to the reader directly using words including "you," "your" and "yours."

Single Spacing: A style of formatting with no blank space between the lines of text.

Subtopic: One of several facets of a supporting topic. The use of subtopics lends organization to the supporting topics of long papers.

Summary: A shorter, simplified version of an original text, rephrased into the writer's own words.

Supporting Topic: A subject that expounds upon the thesis, usually represented in at least one body paragraph.

T-Chart: A method of brainstorming where a chart resembling a capital "T" is written on a large piece of paper. Each side of the vertical line represents a topic and brainstormed points relating to each topic are recorded on the appropriate side.

Thesis Statement: One sentence stating the main argument/theme of the paper. This can be thought of as a one-sentence answer to the prompt.

Topic Sentence: The first sentence of a body paragraph. It should include the subject of the paragraph and how that topic relates to the thesis.

Transition: A word, phrase or sentence that shows the relation between adjacent, different topics.

Venn Diagram: A method of visual brainstorming where two slightly-overlapping circles are drawn on a piece of paper, each circle representing a subject. Brainstormed points relating to each subject are written within the corresponding circle, while points relating to both subjects are written in the overlapping section.

Verb Tense: The way an action is written, indicating when the action took place (in the past, in the present, in the future, etc.).

Volume Number: The number of a grouping of academic journals published within a set period of time.

Works Cited: A section at the end of the paper containing the full details of sources (full citations) for every concrete detail used within the paper.

Appendix VII: References

Bankston, John. *Jack London.* Hockessin: Mitchell Lane Publishers, 2005. Print. Classic Story Tellers.

London, Jack. "To Build a Fire." *The Century Magazine* August 1908. Digital file.

Modern Language Association of America. *MLA Handbook for Writers of Research Papers.* 7th ed. New York: MLA, 2009. Print.

Streissguth, Tom. *Jack London.* Minneapolis: Lerner Publications Company, 2001. Print. Biography.

About the Author

After graduating from Washington State University as a Distinguished Regents Scholar, Danalynn Coulon shifted from student to educator. She has worked as a university-level writing tutor for four years, as a general writing tutor for seven years and as a teacher for many classes and ages. Her specialization is in working with English Language Learner students, which has refined her understanding of the fundamentals of American-style essay writing. Originally from Washington State, Danalynn enjoys hiking, reading and traveling.

83450571R00129

Made in the USA
San Bernardino, CA
25 July 2018